PRAISE FOR SUZY K QUINN

'Suzy brings home the trials and tribulations of being a modern-day wife, mother and sister with great humour.'
—Liza Foreman, *New York Times*

From Suzy's readers on Amazon:

'Lovely read – If there was such a thing as comfort food in book form, this would be it.'

'Amazing, brilliant, funny, a MUST read – Fantastic book, I couldn't put it down (it's now 4.50 a.m.).'

'Well worth five stars – Make yourself feel good about life not being perfect. A smile a minute. Warm and sensitive.'

'Brilliant . . . Just Brilliant – Please, Suzy, keep writing, I am hooked.'

LIES
we tell
MOTHERS

ALSO BY SUZY K QUINN

The Bad Mother Series

Bad Mother's Diary

Bad Mother's Detox

Bad Mother's Holiday

(Prequel) *Bad Mother's Pregnancy*

LIES
we tell
MOTHERS

SUZY K QUINN

LAKE UNION
PUBLISHING

Published by Lake Union Publishing, Seattle

www.apub.com

Amazon, the Amazon logo, and Lake Union Publishing are trademarks of Amazon.com,
Inc., or its affiliates.

ISBN-13: 9781542044677
ISBN-10: 1542044677

Cover design by Lisa Horton

Printed in the United States of America

Truth – there is no birth, only transformation

Contents

PART I: NATURE'S SHIT STORM

#1 LIE – JUST GO WITH YOUR MOTHER'S INSTINCT

They say the darkest hour is just before dawn.

Well, 5 a.m. on that cold Christmas morning was the loneliest, scariest, darkest hour I'd ever experienced.

There I was, sobbing, alone and anxious, wishing some sort of mother's instinct would kick in and tell me what to do.

It was Christmas Day, but our dark, damp apartment did not glow with festive magic.

Save for the single string of cheap tinsel hung over the framed 'Excuse the Mess, We're Alcoholics' print, ours was the apartment Christmas forgot.

Santa hadn't slowed the sledge for us. He kept right on going.

I stood in the blackness, bats beating their wings in my chest, rocking my newborn baby as she cried and cried.

It wasn't working, the rocking. It turns out a wild-eyed, anxious mother on the verge of tears isn't soothing for a baby.

In the winter darkness, I honestly thought I would have a mental breakdown.

Last Christmas Eve, Demi and I had been child-free and living in a big shared house with friends. We'd laughed. We'd celebrated. We'd made interesting cocktails with chocolate liqueur, amaretto and sherry.

This Christmas Eve there was only me, a newborn baby and crippling anxiety.

I had no friends with kids.

No one I could call at 3 a.m. (it's *always* 3 a.m., isn't it?), and I didn't want to wake Demi. He needed energy for my daytime meltdowns.

In the early hours of that dark, lonely morning, Lexi just wouldn't sleep.

I'd done everything.

Fed her.

Fed her again.

Fed her a third time.

Jiggled her around while bending my legs in time to the hokey-cokey. But every time I laid her down . . . *WAAAH!*

I couldn't do this parenting business.

I just couldn't do it.

Yet somehow I had to.

Before I had a baby, I saw myself as a reasonably capable, competent person. And tough too – I mean, I once slept *upright* on a Thai night bus *all* night. But this competent, capable self seemed to have been smashed with a big hammer and set on fire.

If I wasn't a capable, competent adult, who on earth was I?

A frightened, empty shell.

I'd had bad nights before, of course.

The night I first tried cider and threw up into my own hands.

The aforementioned fourteen-hour night-bus ride through Thailand on a non-reclining seat, watching fellow backpackers sleep comfortably on seats that *did* recline.

The night I gave birth, sick and fairground-dizzy on pethidine, listening to other poor labouring women screech things like, 'Jesus H. Christ, I've shat on the bed!'

But *this* was the longest, loneliest, scariest night of my life.

'*If* I survive tonight,' I thought, my inner voice quivering with the drama of it all, 'what about tomorrow night? And the night after that? Surely I won't survive *those*.'

I'd been woken five times since 9 p.m. and Lexi just *wouldn't* fall asleep. It was torture and I was going out of my mind.

On paper, it doesn't sound too bad. Woken up five times? So what? But I was used to a world of light switches and TV remotes; things I could *control*.

Lexi had no 'crying turn off now' switch. No sleepy-time button. In fact, no buttons or operations manual at all.

I was exhausted and stressed to the point of terrified.

Can people die from lack of sleep? I wondered, and the bats doubled their wing-flapping in my chest.

SAS soldiers suffered less, I was quite sure. I mean, they can always *choose* to quit.

Why couldn't I do this? Where was my mother's instinct?

Pre-baby, I had a proper adult, responsible job and believed I was a real proper adult. But during that long, dark Christmas morning, it became horribly apparent that actually . . . well, I wasn't really an adult at all.

Adults don't cry just because they're tired.

Almost overnight, I had become an anxious, hysterical female with the brainpower of a table leg.

I was unable to do simple things like make a cup of tea and remember where I'd left it.

I started enjoying *Big Brother*.

Who was I?

I didn't know it back then, but I was experiencing a transformation of sorts. My old identity – the carefree, child-free, twenty-something 'me' – was being squashed, squeezed and pushed out of existence.

This squeezing and squashing was necessary. It would (eventually) allow me to emerge as a beautiful, sparkly parent butterfly, floating on glittery rainbow wings around small children with a happy, content smile on its older, wiser face.

Most of the time.

Unbeknown to me, I was on a path to happiness. However, back then it didn't feel that way.

You might be wondering who on earth I am and on what authority I champion this identity squashing and squeezing.

Am I a psychologist or something?

Well, no. I'm a fiction writer and I write novels about parenting. I wrote the Bad Mother's Diary series (romantic comedy) and *Don't Tell Teacher* (absolutely not a comedy, unless you have a questionable sense of humour). Oh, and I have two kids.

Really, I'm the last person you can rely on to talk sense. I mean, I spend the day making things up. But there is nothing made up in these pages, because I am way too honest for my own good and frequently overshare.

This is my true story of transformation: how I changed from a free-and-easy twenty- something to a gibbering wreck and then, after a lot of pain, a really, really happy parent.

It was a roller coaster, but roller coasters can be a lot of fun. So let's jump into a wobbly cart together and go on a profound journey. The great, swirly, turny, joyful trip of parenthood.

Strap yourself in – we're in for a bumpy ride.

#2 LIE – PREGNANCY IS *SUCH* A SPECIAL TIME

It all started with pregnancy.

Obviously.

There I was, a normal(ish) late-twenty-something enjoying work and life in the big city. Having fun with my partner and friends. Drinking too much. You know the sort of thing.

Demi and I had recently got married and I felt very lucky to have him. He was (still is) a kind, creative, sensitive fellow who cleans the house and does all our laundry.

> *(Demi – 'I am lucky to have you too. And by the way, I also do the cooking, the washing-up and put out the recycling. Just in case you've forgotten.')*

Suddenly, it dawned on me.

I would be *thirty* soon.

Thirty felt *monumentally* old (ha!). And Demi was no spring chicken either. Come to think of it, *he* was already thirty-three.

Wow.

I realised we should have kids soon, before my womb turned to dust.

Demi was in agreement. He'd wanted to have kids for ages.

Six weeks later, I stood in a shopping-centre toilet cubicle, staring at two pink lines on a pregnancy test.

Pregnant.

I felt . . . well, pretty happy.

We were going to have a little baby!

I was excited to be pregnant, have a giant tummy and get funny cravings for things. I didn't even mind the idea of morning sickness.

Demi was delighted by the news – possibly more delighted than me.

'I will do everything I can to look after you and the baby,' he said.

'Yes, you will,' I replied. 'Or I shall beat you around the head.'

We were *pregnant*.

What a special time. I was extremely grateful to the universe for blessing us (especially considering my alcohol consumption over the summer) and couldn't wait for our little bundle of joy to arrive.

A few weeks later, dark, swirling hormones of doom began whooshing around my body, sweeping away excitement and delight in one big sicky tide.

I felt awful.

Demi and I trotted along to the midwife for our first pre-natal appointment and she gave us the low-down.

There would not be fun times ahead. Only nine months of discomfort, culminating in the agonies of childbirth.

We were duly slapped with a big list of 'Don't dos'.

I couldn't eat raw egg, blue cheese or sushi. I couldn't sleep on my back. I couldn't eat a cinema-size bag of M&Ms without getting heartburn. I couldn't drink alcohol or smoke – well, that was a given. And I wasn't too bothered about the raw egg. But no blue cheese?

I hadn't eaten much blue cheese before I got pregnant. But when I *couldn't* have it . . . why hadn't I eaten more Stilton before?

As pregnancy progressed, I missed more than blue cheese.

I couldn't travel – not really. I was too tired. I couldn't go out to the pub with my friends. I couldn't wear nice clothes. I couldn't walk very far without wanting to sit down.

Things were . . . changing.

This wasn't the special time I'd been promised. It was, in fact, a frightening insight into old age.

I couldn't do half the things I used to *and* I felt weak and tired and needed to be near a toilet.

My life, pre-kids, was exciting. I travelled to Tokyo, Costa Rica, Cambodia and Thailand and had all sorts of crazy jobs while I waited for the big publishing deal I was sure was just around the corner.

I wore bright neon vest tops, skinny jeans and plastic jewellery. I home-dyed blonde and red streaks in my hair.

Me, pre-pregnancy, with my one of my bessie mates, Richie, at a Fat Boy Slim concert during my carefree twenties. Richie looks uncomfortable to have my great bulk on his shoulders, but I'm having a great time.

If you've ever been to Ko Phi Phi in Thailand, you may have visited Big Banana Club. It's a hip-hop bar with a palm-leaf roof and opens out on to the sort of beach you'd expect to see James Bond sauntering along with his latest bikini-model fling.

Before I had kids, one of my crazier side jobs was 'floor filler' at the Big Banana. What's a floor filler? Well, some Thai nightclubs ask sunburnt British travellers to bounce around the dance floor and make their clubs look popular. After all, an empty dance floor is a sad dance floor.

I'm a below-average dancer, but Big Banana had a cure for this: free plastic buckets of SangSom whiskey mixed with Red Bull. They gave me three of these alcoholic mini-buckets during my shift, and hey presto – suddenly I was a FANTASTIC dancer.

Every night, I danced (badly) while sipping from a bucket of amphetamine-laced whiskey and shouting 'Woooo!' And I got paid for it. A pretty good deal, I thought.

My days were free for writing articles and novels (usually with a pounding hangover), eating prawn curry and watching people have bamboo tattoo stakes hammered into their arms.

Good times, right?

For a twenty-something, yes.

I was free, exploring, writing my books and having fun.

After travelling to all sorts of amazing places, I moved back to the UK and carried on with the serious business of failing to get published.

I moved to the city of Brighton and shared a house with lots of friends. Overnight visitors could stay on an unhygienic guest bed in the bathroom ('unhygieno bed'!).

We had fun.

There were parties every weekend, during which we wrote hilarious, philosophical sayings on the kitchen cupboards in wipe-clean marker.

I met my future husband, Demi, at one of these parties (he wrote 'Su is lovely' on a cupboard and it went from there).

Demi and I got together, he moved into the big shared house and we shared a small room overlooking a car park.

We worked really hard – me carving out a career as a writer, Demi in some call-centre hellhole position too boring for me even to remember it and writing songs in his spare time.

After two glorious, fun years, we decided to get married and trotted down to the town hall to apply for a marriage licence.

The registrar asked me questions about Demi's job in case we were marrying for visa purposes.

Registrar: 'What's your partner's job?'

Me: 'Errr . . .'

Registrar: 'This is the person you want to marry. Don't you know his job? Tell us the truth, are you marrying for visa reasons?'

Me: 'Errr . . . look, I'm sorry. Demi's job is too boring to remember. Telephone operative? Phone monkey? We're both UK residents, so . . .'

A few weeks later, we married in a *Star Wars*-themed wedding on Brighton pier.

> *(Demi: 'It wasn't a **Star Wars**-themed wedding, Su. It was general fancy dress. But it just so happened that five Jedis and one Darth Vader turned up. The best man dressed as a giant banana.')*

You see? We were *fun* people.

Demi and me on our wedding day. I am crying with happiness. Demi is apparently laughing at me. Unbeknown to us, life is about to change more than we could ever imagine.

That all changed when I got pregnant.

I didn't realise, back then, that things would never be the same again. Or that it would get worse before it got better.

'Sure, I can't eat blue cheese right now,' I thought as I waddled around in oversized Aerosmith and Guns N' Roses vests. 'I'm pregnant, tired and bored. I don't see my friends much because drinking tequila would be irresponsible. I have to go to bed at 8 p.m. because I need to wake up starving hungry at midnight to drink Heinz tomato soup alone in the dark. But this isn't my *life*. The baby will come out and we'll all have fun again. It'll be *fine*.'

As pregnancy progressed, I felt increasingly sick, frail and old.

I'd never felt so bad in my life, and I've experienced salmonella poisoning, swine flu and some pretty horrendous hangovers.

Most of the time, I had travel-sickness-type nausea that made healthy food upsetting.

I didn't want the midwife-recommended 'vegetable stir-fry'.

I especially didn't want spinach for my iron levels.

The only food I could tolerate was yellow in colour and salted in flavour. I could stretch to orange/brown-coloured food like baked beans and tomato soup if it came in cans and promised to contain absolutely no natural vitamin content.

The midwife told me to eat what I fancied. 'Your body will tell you what it needs,' she said.

I suspected my body didn't 'need' large Big Mac meals, cheese Doritos or cream-topped Starbucks creations, but I indulged heartily in these 'cravings'.

The result? I gained shit loads of weight very early on, which made my lumbering cow of a body even more uncomfortable.

Far from my body telling me what it needed, it gave me terrible advice and made me feel awful.

My mother said ominous things when I got pregnant, like: 'Oh – look out, you're about to feel really ill!' and 'Ho, ho! Watch out for the haemorrhoids, sickness, diarrhoea and thousand other pregnancy symptoms that will turn you into a tired, grumpy invalid and strip away your youth and dignity.'

I didn't pay much attention. What's with all the negativity? Pregnancy is a natural process. It can't be that bad.

Right?

Pre-pregnancy, I pictured my pregnant self the same as my non-pregnant self, except with a large, sticky-out, Mr Greedy stomach tacked on. Maybe having one tiny, girly vomit first thing in the morning.

Nature and I would work in harmony, navigating pregnancy symptoms with good fruit and yoga.

It didn't work out like that.

Me, heavily pregnant and inappropriately sitting next to a beer can. I didn't drink from the beer can, although I'm sure I wanted to.

#3 LIE – YOU'LL BOND WITH YOUR PARTNER MORE THAN EVER

When I first got pregnant, I was confident Demi and I could have a baby *and* carry on living in a big shared house with all our friends.

'It'll be fine,' I said. 'We'll have built-in babysitters. One big, happy, hippy family.'

I wondered why so few other people had kids in shared houses. Surely it was win–win? More love to go around.

Demi thought we should get our own place.

We argued about it.

A lot.

I told Demi he was being small-minded. He told me I was being naive.

After a few months of tired, miserable pregnancy, I had a horrible realisation.

Demi was right.

Our housemates were still living the no-kids, fun, party life. They were staying up late and being really loud. They were having fun without us.

The bastards.

I was going to have to swallow my pride and tell Demi we should move.

Ugh.

Demi was very good about it. He said he thought I might change my mind, so he'd been looking into places and noticed the downstairs apartment was available to rent. Should he schedule in a visit?

It sounded like a great idea.

The downstairs apartment was a little dingy and dark and hadn't been redecorated since the 1960s.

It was part of the same house and called 'The Granny Flat'.

I'm not joking.

Royal Mail labelled post '72 The Granny Flat'. The current residents told us they had terrible trouble explaining to digital TV providers that they didn't need remote controls with extra-large buttons.

The Granny Flat, as you may imagine, boasted spiral-ring hobs that had two settings: 'Off' and 'Bright Red I Burn Things', a shower room with green mould on the ceiling and storage heaters that cost £50 a day to get lukewarm.

There were handles by the front door for wheelchair users and an old fridge that rattled like chattering teeth.

But it was all fine, right? Our own place!

All I saw was a huge bedroom that could fit both a double bed and a cot, plus our very own kitchen, complete with mustard-coloured tiles.

Luxury.

Who needs a functioning cooker and warmth when you have love? We'd make it work somehow!

Even better, we'd be downstairs from all our friends.

Built-in babysitters!

A 'proper' family home didn't occur to us. In the city, entire houses cost a fortune.

It took all afternoon for Demi to move two suitcases of clothes, a few boxes and a bed down from our upstairs room. Yes. *All* afternoon. He kept stopping for tea breaks and chatting to people.

(Demi: 'There were THREE flights of stairs! And I washed the bedroom walls with vinegar solution to remove the nicotine stains, on your instruction.')

I couldn't move anything myself because I was pregnant.

This was infuriating.

Worse, Demi objected to my complaints about his 'slow' pace, because he was doing all the work. He should have counted himself lucky that I didn't pick up that USB cable he'd dropped and start cracking it like a whip.

After Demi (finally) moved our meagre possessions downstairs, I assessed our new living space.

Aside from the bed, we were short of furniture. Actually, devoid of furniture. All we really owned was a wok and a toaster.

Maybe we weren't as grown up as we thought.

'We're nearly thirty and we don't own enough possessions to furnish a home,' I told Demi. 'This is worrying.'

'We own a wok and a toaster and a bed,' said Demi. 'If anything, we're over-furnished.'

'I'm pregnant,' I insisted. 'We need adult furniture. A TV stand. Coffee table. Knick-knacks. And a dining table. Everything is changing and I'm scared. I so desperately want some Stilton!'

Eventually, after a lot of arguing, Demi caved.

'Fine,' he said. 'We'll get some more furniture.'

'But we don't have any money for furniture!'

'People are always throwing stuff out around here,' said Demi. 'We can furnish our home for free.'

In the absence of a better plan, we decided to hit Freecycle and see what we could find. We also decided to keep an eye out for pavement furniture bargains. People in Brighton were always leaving free bits and pieces outside their homes for others to take.

A few days later, I found a solid-wood chest of drawers outside one of Brighton's many identical Victorian terraced houses. It was in amazing condition and I couldn't wait to get home and tell Demi about my free find.

'It's really lovely,' I told Demi. 'I can't believe it's free. And we really need a chest of drawers.'

'Why?'

'Because you keep all your T-shirts in cardboard boxes.'

Demi muttered something about 'nothing wrong with cardboard boxes', saying he'd had some of those boxes since he was eighteen.

I argued about babies and maturity and proper functional furniture.

Luckily, being pregnant, I always had the winning hand. Men are supposed to give pregnant women what they want; otherwise we go mental.

Our kind friend Alex drove us around the city until I finally found the chest of drawers again. To my delight, it was just as lovely as I remembered: solid-wood, varnished and glowing in the late-afternoon sun.

Perfect.

Thank you, cash-rich people of Brighton.

When we got the chest of drawers home and into the bedroom, I noticed the front of the drawers had a sticky quality to them. As if they'd recently been varnished.

'Shit,' I said. 'You don't think this was put out on the street to dry, do you? After someone varnished it?'

We looked over the item, which also had new sawdust shavings clinging to some surfaces and inside the drawers, as if someone had lovingly sanded it down quite recently. Perhaps today.

'That makes sense,' said Demi.

'We need to put it back,' I said. 'Immediately. This is all your fault.'

'But where did we get it from?'

We went back out to look for the house. However, in the maze of Brighton's Victorian terraced streets, one house looks very much like another.

'We can't risk leaving it outside the wrong house,' said Demi. 'That's fly-tipping.'

'So what are we going to do?' I asked.

'We'll have to keep it.'

We still have that chest of drawers and would like to offer sincere apologies to whomever we stole it from. If your newly varnished chest of drawers went missing one sunny Brighton day, please email me and I will pay you for it. And sorry again . . .

With our basic furniture in place, it was time to think about baby equipment. We weren't going to scour Freecycle or the good streets of Brighton for baby stuff – oh no.

I had that 'new parent' urge to make sure everything was totally safe and clean for our precious firstborn child.

A new baby is special and delicate.

(Demi: 'I'd forgotten we were so obsessed with buying brand-new baby stuff. When it came to our second daughter, we were far less fussy. Everything was second-hand. Sorry, Laya.')

The internet offered a handy 'essential baby equipment' checklist:

- Baby bed, cot or crib (check this is European safety standard and measure distance between bars)
- Mattress (you MUST buy this brand-new)

- Swaddle (a controversial item, but babies like being bound up into little parcels – they sleep better that way)
- Eight good-quality bottles
- Breast pump (this will cost you a fortune and fill you with horror)
- Car seat (check and test this BEFORE the birth)
- Large pants (trust me, dear, you'll need these)
- Eight baby sleeping suits
- Eight vests
- Eight day outfits

We saved up and bought what we needed.

Supposedly, our home was now ready for the new arrival.

The huge white cot was wedged by our double bed, ominous and foreboding.

We argued about exactly where the cot should sit – to the left or right of the bed. Then we argued because Demi wanted to paint the bedroom alcoves Arsenal red. Then we argued about whether it makes any difference to put the milk in your tea before or after the boiling water.

(Demi: 'It definitely does.')

I had an uneasy feeling that, far from bonding over parenthood, Demi and I were in for a whole world of arguing and disagreements.

I was right.

Demi and me with wedding guest, brother Richie, at our Brighton Pier wedding. Demi looks thought-ful. Is he full of regret about signing those wedding papers? Too late! You're now legally obliged to spend your life with me.

#4 LIE – ONCE THE MORNING SICKNESS HAS PASSED, YOU'LL FEEL BETTER

As I entered the third trimester, my body unkindly released a lot of crazy-making hormones. Along with feeling old and tired, I started doing out-of-character things like obsessively cleaning bits of the house that didn't need cleaning.

'You're nesting,' people said.

Ugh.

Was I becoming one of those girly girls who carried little puppies in their shoulder bags? If so, this was a very bad time. Surely I needed solid masculine logic to see me through the times ahead? But my body thought differently.

Soon, emotions completely took over. Logic left the building.

At seven months pregnant I was given three bags of second-hand baby clothes by my very kind sister-in-law.

According to the internet, 'baby' needed eight sleeping suits, vests, day outfits, etc.

Simple, right?

So all I had to do was sort through these clothes, extract the required outfits, then give the rest of the clothes away.

The old me would have got on with the job first thing in the morning and had everything in neat piles by 9.30 a.m., leaving time to get on with emails and writing projects.

But something had happened to my organised, logical brain. Mr Spock was long gone, replaced by a gooey, girly, pregnant woman whose heart swelled over all those cute little baby clothes.

Choose *eight* outfits? How could I pick only eight? What about those cute little newborn-baby baseball boots? Impractical, yes, since newborns can't walk. But utterly adorable!

How about that little spotty summer dress – it's just *gorgeous*. Yes, I know I'm having a baby in winter, but does it come in *my* size?

After an hour of sifting through clothes, struggling with the logical, efficient person I used to be and this new, sentimental, girly girl who had leapt out and started singing Judy Garland songs, I had a meltdown.

I phoned poor, long-suffering Demi.

'I can't do this!' I sobbed. 'There are so many clothes and I need to pick eight sleepy suits, but some have short arms and sleeves, and some have long arms and covered feet. And there's some sort of bandana in here and a cowboy outfit. We don't need a cowboy outfit. It's not on the list. BUT I WANT TO KEEP IT, IT'S SO PRETTY!'

Hormones were attacking me. Stripping away my logic and competence, just when I needed those qualities most.

There was a girly girl inside, full of feelings and emotions. But I wasn't ready to meet her yet.

Instead, I got Demi to choose the baby clothes (he dispensed with the cowgirl outfit. I shouted at him. He returned it to the pile) and threw myself into the obsessive preparation recommended by many parenting websites.

I cooked one month's worth of meals in advance, piled up towers of newborn nappies and wet wipes and (bizarrely) scrubbed not only all the internal woodwork, but also the front door.

Having read a website about the danger of germs for newborn babies, I also went steriliser crazy, spraying chemicals all over the place. I googled carpet sterilisers (yes, they exist) before Demi stepped in with some much-needed sanity.

'They had babies in caves years ago, didn't they?' he pointed out. 'Caves have germs. You can't sterilise a cave.'

I agreed that yes, I suppose they did have babies in caves once upon a time. But that was thousands of years ago, and I'm sure if rock steriliser existed back then any *decent* mother would have used it.

'You don't even care about germs,' said Demi. 'Remember when you ate that two-months-out-of-date Covent Garden Soup because you'd paid £3 for it and didn't want to see it wasted? You said a few germs were good for you.'

Demi was right – I never usually worried about germs or bothered myself with the names and purposes of cleaning products.

But I wasn't myself. The hormones were taking over.

I don't know why they call this obsessive behaviour nesting – I doubt birds go mad for cleaning products or sterilise their claws.

It felt like a storm was coming and I had to stock up with supplies and batten down the hatches or risk being washed away.

Once the baby came, I envisaged Demi and me captive in our own home for those dreaded 'first three months'. After that, I thought life would snap back to normal.

I really, honestly thought that.

#5 LIE – JUST BREATHE THROUGH IT

We're a long way from nature these days, aren't we? Have you noticed? In our lovely, climate-controlled little boxes, cars, homes, offices and trains, we spend a lot of our lives well clear of that cruel and uncomfortable beast they call nature.

You're probably sitting in one of these boxes right now, I imagine. Unless you're lucky enough to be on a holiday sun lounger by a swimming pool. In which case, have a beer for me.

Anyway, I have a theory about Mother Nature. I think she's annoyed that we continually sidestep her wondrous planet of miracles.

'Look, I made that beautiful forest glade for you,' she's saying. 'And where's my thanks? You want to sit inside a hunk of cement, consuming poor imitations of my life's work. Sunny Delight orange-*flavour* drink? What IS that?'

But she gets her own back with pregnancy and labour.

'You can't sidestep this, dearie!' (I'm imagining Mother Nature a bit like the wicked witch in *Snow White* here.) 'You must accept your fate! Nature is pain!'

Pre-labour, I was certain I would bypass the trauma of childbirth. Everything can be fixed, right? Solved. *Controlled*. As long as you put in the hard work and preparation.

There was a lot of information on the world wide web that suggested I could have a pain-free birth if I did things the right way.

Women *do* have easy labours, the internet told me. There were YouTube videos to prove it, and I watched them. Lovely, serene women dressed in flowing white robes, taking deep breaths in birthing pools.

I bought a book on hypnobirthing and reassured myself that human beings are designed to give birth. It's natural. And nature designs everything very well.

Demi was called forth to help me design a birth plan.

There were so many lovely options. Almost like a wedding. You could have your baby in a big warm pool of water at home, surrounded by candles and your choice of music. It sounded delightful.

I couldn't wait.

We (I) eventually decided to have the baby at home 'where nature intended' and piled up second-hand towels for the litres of bodily fluid that would apparently ruin our carpet.

I did all the hypnobirthing exercises from the book, practising deep breathing and relaxing and releasing. I frequently called to mind the charming hypnobirthing story of the Victorian woman who gave birth in a dank Victorian alleyway with no pain relief.

Plenty of women rocked this labour business and I would too. This was going to be a pain-free, easy-peasy experience – yes indeed.

Right?

(Demi: 'At this stage, I already suspected labour would be difficult. One of my friends was a new father and had the thousand-yard stare of a haunted man. He described suction cups. Forceps. I've been in the Cypriot army. I know trauma when I see it.')

I even told Demi, *it's OK*. All I have to do is breathe properly and it'll all be fine. No big deal. I'm tough. I got to the third round in that chilli challenge, remember? I only pulled out when those Carolina Reaper-coated tortilla chips gave me full-body convulsions.

I was looking forward to labour, actually. A bit of a challenge and/or completely pain-free.

Just breathe through it!

However, one hypnobirthing book could not undo a lifetime of manic overthinking.

It would take longer than nine months to reboot my personality and make me a calm earth mother. But I didn't realise that back then.

As the due date drew nearer, Demi and I joined an antenatal class called You To Us.

(Demi: 'I only just got that – you-to-us, UTERUS! Clever.')

Unlike mainstream NCT classes, You To Us was a more laid-back class with a natural birthing ethos and beanbags on the floor.

During our first class, our teacher (who looked exactly like Zoë Wanamaker) showed us a simulated contraction over a birthing ball. She was a fine actress and drew out the contraction for the full minute – the time we could expect during *real* birth.

A few would-be parents went pale.

Then pictures were passed around – babies coming out of vaginas. We're talking real close-ups.

One father laughed – the kind of hysterical laugh that suggested he'd never considered his wife's special place being ripped in two and he wasn't coping well with the idea.

We gripped ice cubes to get our heads around breathing through labour pains, and also had a bang of some real gas and air – just to try it out.

Fun stuff, and if you live in Brighton I highly recommend this class.

The other soon-to-be-mothers were as fed up as I was to be heavily pregnant, but they were lovely and we all got along. Top of the discussion was due dates – who was first in line? Who would pop first?

My due date came and I was ready to go.

Let's do this thing.

Let's have this baby.

Bring it on.

#6 LIE – AT 40 WEEKS, YOU'RE OVERDUE

Of course, nothing happened on my due date.

As a punctual person, I was shocked.

What was going on?

People phoned and asked if the baby had arrived.

'No!' I snapped. 'Not even the tiniest little twinge of a contraction. But the baby isn't *late*, actually. I've just googled it. Only one per cent of women give birth on their due date. They're the anomaly, not me. You're *not overdue* at forty weeks.'

I've never been a patient person. Imagine a really, really impatient person waiting for a turtle to cross a lawn with life-saving medicine on its back, and you'll get a sense of how uncomfortable I felt when my due date passed.

Research told me that there is no such thing as overdue. It's a nonsense made up by the hospital. Why, in France you're not overdue until you're 42 weeks pregnant! My logical brain knew that. But I also knew I wanted this baby out as soon as possible and, in medical language, it was *overdue*.

I'd love to say that my impatience was because I couldn't wait to see my baby, but that would be a lie. What I couldn't wait to do was sit in a chair for more than half an hour without getting bum pain, sleep all night long without waking (ha!), and eat a huge great big block of Stilton.

Mum recommended I take my mind off things by 'boning up' for the big day and reading baby books. She hadn't read a single baby book before giving birth to twin girls (my sister and me) and regretted it.

I was appalled.

Fancy not reading a single baby book before having twins!

I'd read at least ten books already, asked Google hundreds of questions and pegged my political parenting flag to the 'sleep training' movement.

My favourite baby book, I told Mum, was a sleep-training manual advocating forward planning and a strict baby schedule.

The book promised I could turn my baby into an efficient sleeping and feeding machine within three months and sidestep the many agonies of early parenthood.

This sounded perfect.

'I'll put the baby down for a three-hour nap after lunch and get a little work done,' I said.

Mum laughed.

The sleep-training book had a deceivingly gentle name like *Bringing up Calm Little Darling Babies*, but in my mind I called it *Parenting for Control Freaks*. This is in no way meant to insult the author, who has been the saviour of many mothers and who offers sound, solid baby advice. But *my* needs from this book wandered into the dark side of the force. The control-freaky, scared-of-the-unknown, 'Luke I Am Your Father' side.

(Demi: 'I read this book too because you made me. I can sum it up in four words: this woman is nuts.')

It wasn't that I minded hard work when the baby came. But I very, very much needed to know exactly what and when that hard work would be. Sleep-training advice assured me this kind of control could be mine.

By the last trimester, I'd already memorised sleep schedules and mentally rehearsed those 'first three months', during which I'd have to wake up at 6 a.m. (totally fine – I already do!), feed, work during nap times and go to bed at 9 p.m. (a bit boring, but it won't be forever).

Baby would slot into life. Life would go on as before, except now we'd have a lovely little baby to look after and even more love in our lives.

With the appropriate tools and preparation, I was sure this brave new world of parenthood could be mastered and controlled. It was just a matter of putting in the hard work.

I'd taken the precaution of printing out a 'baby schedule' and pinning it behind the door of the new wardrobe of baby clothes, quietly humming to myself as I imagined the well-oiled machine of parenthood.

I'd also followed the advice (and it was good advice) to put together the breast pump, work out the baby car seat, etc., before the birth.

Parenting for Control Freaks didn't tell me exactly why I should do this, but I enjoyed all the unboxing and messing around with the new toys.

I now know mastering equipment, pre-baby, is essential. Once you've had a baby, the only thoughts you can manage are: 'If I've fed the baby at 11 a.m. and it needs feeding three hours later, what time will it be?' And: 'Where did I leave that cup of tea?'

I was a swotty head girl preparing for a baby exam and confidently expecting an A.

Of course, I knew there'd be a tough induction. After all, baby schedules, if you've ever read one, are pretty ruthless. Many of them don't factor in things like showering, indecision or popping to Starbucks for a fancy hot chocolate.

For anyone who hasn't read a baby sleep-training schedule, it goes something like this:

6.30 a.m. – Express breast milk using a breast pump, then drink a large glass of water.
7 a.m. – Feed baby.

8.10 a.m. – Eat breakfast and drink another large glass of water.

8.30 a.m. – Wash and sterilise breast pump.

9 a.m. – Dress baby and yourself.

9.30 a.m. – Stimulate baby.

11 a.m. – Feed baby.

11.30 a.m. – Prepare lunch.

12 p.m. – Have a large glass of water.

12.10 p.m. – Put baby to sleep.

12.30 p.m. – Have your lunch, shower, tidy house and wash breakfast things.

2 p.m. – Feed baby.

2.30 p.m. – Put baby to sleep.

5 p.m. – Feed baby.

5.30 p.m. – Bath baby.

6.30 p.m. – Feed baby.

7 p.m. – Put baby to sleep.

7.30 p.m. – Eat dinner.

8 p.m. – Mother go to bed.

YOU WILL NOT HAVE TIME TO PREPARE DINNER, SO FREEZE THREE MONTHS' WORTH OF MEALS BEFOREHAND!

The reality is more like this . . .

6.30 a.m. – Express milk alone in a dark room, the mechanical whirring of the breast pump haunting the dreams of your sleeping partner.

6.45 a.m. – Baby begins to stir. Panic! Baby should NOT be fed until 7 a.m. Watch baby, filled with anxiety, wondering how long you can suffer her little bleating cries before picking her up.

7 a.m. – You did it! You held off until 7 a.m. Breast-feed baby, feeling ravenously thirsty yourself and wondering the whole time how much milk your baby is getting, and if you've possibly stolen some of her milk by expressing earlier. WHY don't they build babies with see-through stomachs so you can SEE if they're full? And can I reach that glass of water? Can I reach it? No, not quite. Oh shit. I just knocked the water over.

7.15 a.m. – Baby has stopped feeding! The schedule said she should take HALF AN HOUR. Is she full enough? Has the milk run out?

7.16 a.m. – Change baby whilst experiencing heart-palpitating anxiety.

7.30 a.m. – Partner gives you a big hug and makes you feel better. Brings you a glass of water (he's so lovely!) but you don't feel thirsty now so you don't bother with it. You will later learn that was a mistake.

7.45 a.m. – Are you going to bother getting dressed yet? You'd have to shower first and that's tiring. Oh, you should shower. Come on, it's been days.

8.10 a.m. – Eat as many sugary carbohydrates as you can get your hands on.

8.30 a.m. – Look at the unwashed breast pump, hating it with a passion and knowing that you are not cut out for nursing or midwifery.

9 a.m. – Sort through the pile of assorted hand-me-downs and impulse 'Oh that's so pretty for my new baby!' purchases, trying to find something suitable for your baby to wear. Settle on the same thing you always do: any outfit that's clean and easy to take off and on.

9.30 a.m. – Why is the baby crying? Is she hungry? I'd better feed her just in case.

11 a.m. – Feed baby. Already? But I just fed her! Oh my GOD, I'm thirsty. Where's the water? I can't reach it. Gah! Trapped under baby.

11.30 a.m. – Baby has fallen asleep while feeding. This is NOT part of the schedule – she's not supposed to sleep until noon. Should I wake up baby? No – don't be a fool. Watch The Real Housewives of Orange County *while you have the chance.*

12 p.m. – Look at the large glass of water you're supposed to drink. You're not all that thirsty any more. Decide you'd rather have hot chocolate and a handful of M&Ms.

12.10 p.m. – Baby still sleeping. Aaah, so peaceful. Time for more TV.

12.30 p.m. – Eat more sugary carbohydrates and stare at all the things you should be tidying and washing. Thank the lord you have a modern, domesticated partner who washes up and does laundry. How on earth did your own mother manage?

2 p.m. – Baby still sleeping. She should be feeding right now. Try to wake baby, but baby is not having any of it.

2.30 p.m. – Baby still sleeping. More TV. Partner tells you he's happy you're resting and that you look more beautiful than ever and is there anything he can get for you? A cup of tea or even more chocolate cake? Tell him to keep his voice down, and what did that 'happy you're resting' comment mean? Is he calling you lazy? The cheek of it!

5 p.m. – Baby awake! Feed baby.

5.30 p.m. – Baby now crying non-stop and nothing you do can calm her down. Torture.

7 p.m. – Try to put baby to bed, but she screams to be held and won't be put down.

7.30 p.m. – Try to eat a microwaveable lasagne while jiggling and rocking baby, taking it in turns with your partner. However, HE isn't doing it right. Your stressed, sleep-deprived brain is quite sure about that. No, give her to ME. You're doing it all wrong.

8 p.m. – Baby finally falls asleep.

9 p.m. – Baby wakes to feed.

11 a.m. – Baby wakes to feed.

3 a.m. – Baby wakes to feed.

5 a.m. – Baby wakes to feed.

I'd be a bit bored during the newborn phase, of course, but I would cope because it would only last three months.

Or maybe two.

Lovely.

I would be myself again – with a baby strapped casually to my back (making no noise whatsoever and definitely not being sick into my hair).

Babies can travel on buses, can't they? And planes?

My mum had an extra good laugh when I told her about my efficient, printed baby schedule and forward planning. She said ominous things like, 'You'll learn.' And: 'Seven o'clock put baby to sleep! Just like that! Ha ha ha! You might want to add "Rock the baby back and forth for two hours!"'

But what did she know? Mum had *twin* babies. She can barely remember any of it – it was way too traumatic.

Mum is always telling me she'd rather have gone to prison during the first year of motherhood, because at least she would have had tea breaks. She stops women with twin babies in the street, puts a pitying hand over theirs and says, 'I know. It's *awful*, isn't it?'

For my dad, the newborn phase was so bad that he blotted it out of his memory entirely. When I asked him how often newborn babies feed, he said: 'Oh, quite a lot. At least once a day.'

You see? Not a clue.

Of *course*, babies were hard work in the 1970s, when everything was a stimulating orange colour and no one could afford disposable nappies. Also, the *Parenting for Control Freaks* book wasn't around back then.

Mum and Dad holding me and my twin sis in the 1970s, before disposable nappies or Bumbos. They were legends. Note how unhappy me and my sis look, though. I've never seen a baby that young frowning before. Clearly we hadn't followed any sort of sleep-training routine.

When I reached a week and a half 'overdue', the midwives got itchy feet. They called me in for an invasive internal examination called a 'sweep'.

'Sweep'. Such an innocent word, isn't it?

Just a little 'sweep' around to get things moving.

One of the many medical maternity terms that hide a world of unpleasantness. Other innocent-sounding words include 'induction pessary', 'ventouse' and 'crowning'.

I had no clue what a sweep was until they hauled me up on the midwife's paper-covered table and started stretching my vagina around like an elastic band. Naively, I'd assumed it would be a delicate procedure, but I was beginning to learn that in the world of babies, vaginas are not treated gently. They are no longer a fun part of the body, but a tough and durable object that will soon be ripped open and stitched up.

After the sweep, the midwife told me that lots of women go into labour within 24 hours of vaginal interference.

'Maybe those women were about to go into labour anyway,' I suggested. 'Since you do the sweeps when women are well past their due date.'

'Who knows?' said the midwife. 'Birth is a very mysterious, very under-researched topic. But belt and braces. Eat some pineapple and spicy curry too. Many women go into labour after eating them.'

'Could this also be because they're past their due date and about to go into labour anyway?'

'Who knows?'

At two weeks overdue, the hospital decided I needed to be induced.

I was not happy about this. After all, there were so many horror stories about inductions. Even the hospital described them as more painful. Longer. More likely to lead to 'interventions' (which also sounded painful).

However, after waiting weeks for something to happen and fielding the many 'has the baby come yet' phone calls from well-meaning family and friends, I'd had enough of slow, lazy, poorly designed nature.

'Let's do the induction,' I told Demi. 'I'm sure I can manage the extra induction pain. Labour is all about breathing. You just breathe through it.'

The night before the induction, I waddled into town for a nice meal with Demi. Our last supper, as it were. We chose a curry place, obviously. I was certain that one last shit-hot curry would bring on labour. Absolutely certain.

I didn't tell Demi, but I'd booked the induction as a double bluff. I thought if I chilled out a bit and gave my body an actual baby date, it might get on and go into labour all by itself that night. I'd heard stories of such things.

'This will be the last evening you'll enjoy yourself for a while,' my mum said in that ominous tone you hear at the beginning of horror movies.

'Enjoy myself?' I said. 'I'm uncomfortably pregnant, mildly incontinent and can't get comfortable in any position for more than thirty minutes. AND curry gives me heartburn. I will enjoy myself much more when the baby comes out. Which it might do tonight. I intend to order the hottest curry they have AND extra chillies. Plus, I'm bringing my own pineapple for dessert.'

#7 LIE – SPICY CURRY AND PINEAPPLE BRING ON LABOUR

After our 'last supper' of mega-burny curry and a whole pineapple, I went to bed and waited for labour to happen.

It didn't.

Indigestion happened. A little bit of flatulence happened. Labour remained a shy maiden, too coy to show her face.

So that was that.

The next morning, Demi and I took the bus to hospital for the induction.

It was baby time. Well, induction time at least and, in my naivety, I thought this meant baby would come quickly now. Twelve hours max.

I was quite excited. It felt romantic, passing through the city and thinking wistfully, 'The world will never look the same again. Today is the day I'll have my baby.'

I was wrong about that last part.

The baby wouldn't come today. But in that poetic moment, I had no idea of the horrors to come.

At the labour ward, we were led to the 'induction area'.

We watched other induction victims stagger around, grey-faced and wrung out, amid the animalistic cries of labouring women.

From somewhere deep within the bowels of the labour ward, a woman screeched, 'It's like shitting a watermelon!'

A midwife arrived, swept back the curtain and asked me to remove my underwear – as midwives tend to do.

'I need to insert the pessary,' said the midwife.

'What pessary?' I asked.

'The induction pessary,' said the midwife.

'Is that all the induction is?' I asked. 'A tablet shoved in my vagina?'

'Yes.'

I was disappointed. I'd imagined something much more full-on, involving syringes or possibly a drip.

The midwife shoved a scratchy, white tampon-type thing into my vagina and off she went, throwing these words over her shoulder: 'The pain won't start for a few hours. Sleep if you can. But not on your back – it's dangerous.'

I tried to sleep as agonised, labouring screams cut the air, but couldn't. It was like trying to rest in a war zone.

Demi suggested we take a tour of the hospital while we waited for things to 'kick off'.

'Yes,' I said. 'Let's see what kind of food they do. I've heard there's a Subway sandwich concession. And a Starbucks.'

Ah, the simple joys of child-free people.

Demi and I walked around the grounds, noticed and approved of the Starbucks, assessed possible lunch options and tried to forget the awful scenes we'd seen and heard upstairs. That wouldn't be *me*. I'd *handle* things. It was all about deep breathing and staying calm.

One jumbo hot chocolate with cream and a toffee nut latte later, I experienced strong waves across my stomach that made me need to sit down. They lasted a minute or so and were warm and in no way unpleasant.

I naively assumed these were contractions, which (following advice from the hypnobirthing book) I'd decided to call 'interesting sensations'.

Thank goodness.

I *knew* things wouldn't be that bad.

Then the waves started to build. And build.

It's hard to remember what happened next because time stopped being a nice, familiar line that moves forward and became snatches of mismatched moments.

I remember pacing around a bed, orange flashes before my eyes, being sick into cardboard cowboy hats and thinking it was a shame to waste that £2.70 toffee nut latte and £2.90 hot chocolate with cream.

> *(Demi: 'I held those cardboard cowboy hats of sick on my lap for an hour. Eventually, I chanced putting them on the windowsill. A midwife materialised out of thin air and shouted at me about incorrect procedures with clinical waste.')*

Suddenly it was night-time – a foreboding backdrop.

'I must only be an hour away from the pushing bit,' I remember telling Demi. 'The average labour time is twelve hours. Has it been twelve hours? I always do things quickly.'

Then a midwife came.

'How long until the baby comes?' I asked. 'Can you give me a time? I know everyone says they can't be exact, but can you be approximate? What percentage of labour have I done already?'

'You're not *in* labour yet,' said the midwife.

'Not in labour?' I was confused. 'How can I not be in labour? I've been having contractions all day.'

'Those aren't contractions,' said the midwife. 'They're sensations brought on by the induction pessary. Nothing is happening. You're not dilating at all.'

'When will I start dilating?' I asked.

'It could be days.'

'Days?' I gibbered. 'I can't be in pain like this for days. How will I sleep?'

'You probably won't sleep,' said the midwife matter-of-factly. 'And definitely not when the contractions start. That's *real* pain.' She pinged off her rubber gloves and handed me three more cardboard cowboy hats. 'You'll probably vomit more when things get really bad. Mind the sheets – we've got a laundry issue. Our usual company isn't collecting.'

'Can I have an epidural now?' I asked.

'No.'

You know that bit on a roller coaster where the train cranks up, up, up, then hesitates on the crest of the track so you can fully absorb the eye-watering terror of the sheer drop? That's how I felt at that moment – trapped under a big metal bar that I had no power to release.

It wasn't the pain that was so scary. It was the lack of escape routes. I was strapped in and couldn't get off.

The induction was exactly that – an induction to motherhood. Training for things to come, i.e. inescapable fear and responsibility.

Birth was transforming me. I was leaving my party days behind and becoming a grown-up. But I didn't know it yet.

#8 LIE – CHILDBIRTH ISN'T THAT BAD . . .

My long night of 'labour that wasn't really labour' went on. And on. And on.

As dawn broke, a midwife came for the usual rummage around and checked the baby's heartbeat.

I waited for the inevitable bad news that I still wasn't in labour. But the midwife didn't say anything. Instead, she looked worried.

Suddenly, all the lights came on.

A doctor appeared.

'Hello, Mrs Quinn,' said the doctor. 'It's nothing to worry about, but the baby's heartbeat is dropping and we're concerned it might die.'

Whoa.

Who'd have thought I could feel even worse than I did already?

Given the seriousness of this situation, I decided to forgo my usual annoyance at being called 'Mrs' when I prefer 'Ms'.

The doctor suggested I have a C-section (well, *told* me really, but dressed it up as a suggestion).

'A C-section?' I said. 'As in, you'd cut me open and take the baby out immediately?'

'Yes,' said the doctor.

'Let's roll.'

They took this instruction literally and wheeled me into a surgical theatre, where I was given a full-spinal anaesthetic. Then they sprayed me with cold water to make sure it had taken effect, got a big, human-spatula-type thing and shovelled me on to an operating table.

(Demi: 'I was ushered into a room and given scrubs. Minutes later, I emerged as Doctor Demi, a bit like Stars In Their Eyes *without the smoke.')*

Demi appeared, wearing a silly green surgical mask and making bad jokes about George Clooney.

Then the surgeon said I'd feel some 'sensations' in my stomach, 'like someone doing the washing-up'.

Ho, ho, ho.

A little mini stomach screen was erected to spare me the horror of watching my own major abdominal surgery.

There was a lot of tugging and pulling, and then a blood-streaked giant baked potato was placed on my chest.

A baby! A wrinkly, angry, red-lipped baby!

I observed this miracle of nature. How did this work, then?

Lexi soon gave me a demonstration. She started to cry.

The surgeon gave the nurse a knowing nod, and we were swiftly turfed out into the hallway. We were left out there for a long time – probably too long by hospital standards – but I didn't mind.

Lexi was just fascinating.

The hormonal, singing Judy Garland figure resurfaced – probably due to the morphine I'd been given.

It was all a bit full-on having major surgery and then being responsible for a baby as a totally amateur parent, but in that moment I was OK. As I say, morphine really is very good.

Demi was there sometimes, gone at others. I was never sure why, and it didn't matter.

> *(Demi: 'You told me to go home and sleep on a proper bed and ring all our family and put photos on Facebook, then come back with Doritos and hot chocolate.')*

Everything was just lovely.

Then the painkillers started to wear off.

Me, having just given birth to Lexi. I'm a cross between 'adoring mother looking at new baby' and 'just about to yawn'. Lexi clearly doesn't quite trust me just yet.

#9 LIE – BREAST IS BEST

Before I gave birth, I thought I had a decision to make: should I breast-feed or not?

Here is the truth – I did not make a decision. I was put under HUGE societal and medical pressure to breastfeed.

I was not one of the lucky ones who had some guilt-free medical reason not to breastfeed (the baby wouldn't latch on, milk wouldn't come through properly, etc.). Sorry if you couldn't breastfeed and wanted to, by the way, but ultimately you may have dodged a bullet.

The moment Lexi was born, I tried to encourage her to 'latch on'. And I mean literally the moment she was born. They put her on my chest, having just cut my stomach open, and I whacked out a boob and encouraged her to have a go.

I didn't even consider bottle-feeding. After all, it had been drummed into me for years – breast is best.

After being wheeled into the corridor outside the operating theatre, I tried over and over again to get Lexi feeding. Eventually, she did it. I was delighted.

The midwives came past and said encouraging things like, 'Oh, he's really getting the hang of that, isn't he?'

'It's a girl!' I'd tell them gaily as they hurried away down the corridor.

Eventually, someone came to push me up to the postnatal ward. When we got there, my spinal epidural began to wear off and I felt quite keenly that my whole stomach had been cut open a few hours ago. Not only that, I was now in charge of a tiny baby.

This was worrying.

I'd never had hospital treatment before, let alone a major operation. And obviously I'd never cared for anything as vulnerable and needy as a newborn.

Anxiety began to build.

I asked the midwives question after question: 'How will I know if the baby has got any milk out of my boobs? Is there a way to measure? Can we X-ray her stomach or something? Is she sleeping for too long? Should I start timing her sleep? Should I use one boob or two or what?'

You know – *necessary* questions.

The midwives gave vague, non-committal answers like 'follow baby's lead'. Or, worse, they answered questions I hadn't actually asked with universal truisms like, 'Baby will be OK. They're designed to survive!'

The only viable piece of advice was an ominous: 'Don't feed for *too* long or you'll get very sore.'

They were right about that. After a day of breastfeeding, my boobs were in agony.

Have you ever had a blister but kept walking in the same shoes? My boobs felt like that, but I couldn't take those wretched shoes off.

Once upon a time, when we lived naked in caves, boobs endured all the elements and were tough as old bootstraps. They could handle a baby's gums, no problem. But modern living, clothes, bras and so forth had softened me. My boobs were spoiled little princesses, overly cosseted by clothing and an indoor lifestyle. They'd been wrapped in cotton wool and turned into weaklings. They weren't fit for purpose.

By day two, my boobs were so sore that even the most hardened midwife (the one with bad breath) took pity on me. She wheeled out the old Ford Fiesta-sized milk-pumping machine so I could get milk out of my boobs without (as much) pain.

Thirty minutes of (only slightly less painful) boob pumping extracted enough milk to cover the bottom of a teaspoon.

It was all so undignified, sitting around like a big docile cow, listening to the whirring motor pump making its weird donkey noises.

'I don't think I want to breastfeed, actually,' I told the midwife as blood began appearing in the milk-collection thingy. 'The pain is awful and seems to be getting worse.'

'Well, yes,' said the midwife. 'You have no time to heal, you see. Because you have to keep feeding.'

'I'd like to switch to formula,' I decided, my voice rising. 'This has all been a dreadful mistake.'

'You can't do that now you've started breastfeeding,' said the midwife. 'Babies won't take to a bottle once they've had breast. They call it nipple confusion. Breast is best. YOU CAN'T CHANGE YOUR MIND.'

'When will the pain stop?' I asked, tears in my eyes.

'It'll get worse before it gets better,' said the midwife. 'Your real milk hasn't come in yet.'

'What? Not *real* milk? What is this stuff coming out then?'

'Colostrum. It's pre-milk, just to keep the baby going.'

'So what happens when the real milk comes in?' I asked.

'When the milk comes in, she'll be feeding for much longer. So . . . it'll probably hurt more.'

Hurt more than this?

Oh good god.

Prior to breastfeeding, I'd been spoiled by my range of movements. Even after abdominal surgery, I could still reach for a cup of tea or a bag of peanut M&Ms. Manage the occasional hobble to the toilet for a terrifying 'try' at a bowel movement.

Now, any movement of my giant, sore cow udders brought waves of pain. Bras and clothing were right out. I had to hang out in hospital topless. What on earth was I going to do when they let me out on Civvy Street?

I couldn't walk around Brighton with no top on. It was winter.

Before I had a baby, I had a scientific, computer-like view of breastfeeding. Baby goes on, milk comes out. Baby is full of milk, doesn't need feeding for three, maybe four hours.

Oh, no, no, no.

This, I quickly realised, was *not* how things worked.

Baby goes on, boobs are in agony. Baby comes off. Why has baby come off? It's only been a minute!

Baby has fallen asleep. Baby has woken up and is now feeding again. Demi arrives at hospital and offers to take baby for a walk, since she's 'just fed'.

Scream at Demi, 'But it's all so unpredictable! Yes, she's just fed now, but she might need another feed in ten minutes. I don't know anything any more! I can't even leave her side! And it hurts so much!'

As I was feeling sorry for myself, a new mother moved into the next bed with her newborn baby. She was only a teenager, poor thing, and looked terrified.

Within minutes, a midwife clipped over. She drew the curtain around the girl's bed as if to 'dampen' their private interview, but we could hear everything.

'How are you planning on feeding this baby?' the midwife asked.

'Milk?' the girl replied nervously, sensing a trick.

'From a bottle?'

'Ye-es?'

'So you won't be *trying* breastfeeding?' The midwife's words were laden with disapproval.

'No.'

There was a collective intake of breath around the ward.

'Breastfeeding really is much better for the baby,' the midwife continued.

'My mum says it'll be hard enough as it is,' the girl whispered.

'Oh, breastfeeding isn't difficult,' the midwife lied. 'In many ways, it's *easier* than bottles. No washing-up!'

I lay beside the girl, my boobs literally bleeding, wondering if it was fair to pressure everyone into breastfeeding.

I mean, yes – some women love doing it. Not all women find it painful. I have seen many a calm, dreamy-faced mother having a lovely time feeding her baby.

But some of us have a really hard time, especially if we've already been through a difficult, tiring labour.

Maybe what a baby really needs is a happy, smiling mother – not one wincing in pain and shouting at her partner, 'It's always me! ALWAYS me! I get no days off, no nights off. I NEVER get a break!'

When the bad-cop midwife left, I whispered to the girl: 'Good for you. Make up your own mind.'

The girl started to cry. 'I don't think I can do this,' she said. 'I'm too young.'

'Age has nothing to do with it,' I reassured her. 'None of us knows what we're doing. I'm nearly thirty and completely terrified.'

And it was true. Especially as the time drew nearer to leave the hospital.

Being incompetent around a team of qualified midwives was one thing. Being incompetent at home, with a major surgical incision and no morphine, was quite another.

#10 LIE – YOUR NEW BABY WILL TELL YOU WHAT IT NEEDS

After three days in hospital, the midwives decided I was well enough to take Lexi home.

They judged this on one simple question: 'Have you been for a poo?'

Yes. Yes, I had.

Well, to be precise, I'd staggered to the toilet that morning and done the longest fart ever as unbelievable quantities of air left my body. (If you've ever had abdominal surgery, you'll know exactly what I mean.) Then, very tentatively, I chanced a poo, clinging on to the toilet seat and terrified that I might shit my insides into the bowl.

I didn't feel well enough to go home. Not at all. My intestines felt like they were falling out whenever I rolled over, and I was lying around topless due to breastfeeding agony.

But the hospital needed the bed, so it was time to go.

'Don't worry,' said the midwives. 'You'll be fine. Baby will tell you what she needs.'

Taking Lexi home from hospital should have been a joyful day, but I didn't feel all that joyful. In fact, the godawful grey wintery weather matched my mood perfectly.

(A lot of writers are obsessed with the weather – the howling bleak winds, lashing grey rain, etc. We're a pretentious bunch and I am no exception.)

Leave the lovely, sterile hospital environment with its nice painkillers and wipe-clean surfaces? Without the professional expertise of the midwives, bad breath or otherwise? How would we cope?

Lexi was awfully cute, with her downy head, little hands and so on. I enjoyed looking at her, holding her close and so forth. But I was also in a lot of pain and . . . well . . . scared.

I didn't have that soft, loving face you see on new parents – you know the one. 'I'm in love with this precious new life' eyes, teamed with a soft 'tired but blissfully happy' smile.

When I looked in the mirror, I saw the vulnerable female lead in a horror movie.

I looked terrified.

I had no clue how to care for this baby. Lexi absolutely did not tell me what she needed. She just cried, which could mean anything. Hungry? Uncomfortable? Angry because Demi dressed her in an Arsenal baby outfit? Who knew?

(Demi: 'You said you liked that outfit!')

You know those teachers at school? The harassed ones who aren't really coping. The teachers you know you can mess around (sorry we did that, Mrs Taylor). That's how I looked.

Overwhelmed, overworked and afraid.

How would I cope out in the wild?

When it was time to leave the hospital, Mum and Dad came to visit. They offered to drive me and the new baby home, since Demi and I were too cosmopolitan (and immature) to own a car.

It was very kind of them.

And maybe they could help me interpret Lexi's cries. Crack the baby code. Get some proper communication going so Lexi could actually tell me what was wrong.

Pre-kids, I had a very separate life from my parents.

We lived in different places, knew different people, had different interests – everything.

I didn't care to visit historical English towns and ponder exactly when that castle was built, then have a nice cup of tea and a buttery slice of cake. And Mum and Dad didn't shout 'TUUUUNE!' to drum-and-bass music, drink beer on stony Brighton beach or try experimental cider flavours at music festivals.

My parents live in my home town of Colchester, Essex – a lovely historic place with a castle and authentic chunks of Roman wall, and the proud documentary subject of *Squaddie Town: Do Essex Girls Sleep Around?*

Brighton, on the other hand, had no Roman wall whatsoever – just a bunch of quirky, colourful little knick-knack shops, vegetarian restaurants and pubs with ironic, cool names like 'The Office'.

Let me tell you a little bit about my parents.

My mum is a trailblazing feminist who worked full-time WITH BABY TWINS AT HOME, while renovating a house and still finding time to be a political campaigner. She enjoys wholemeal bread, cycling in the countryside while wearing a high-visibility jacket, and doing community garden projects. She was head girl at her school.

Dad, on the other hand, went to juvenile detention as a teenager for letting all the animals out of a zoo. He is absolutely unable to follow rules and will often walk on the road, just because the rule is he should be on the pavement. He puts on really fun, popular events in parks, is extremely generous and makes extravagant, dairy-rich meals – often cooking twice as much food as is needed. He is very big-hearted and kind and has so many friends that it's impossible to walk anywhere with him in a timely fashion because he gets stopped every five minutes.

Here is my dad, featured in the local paper after resuscitating a homeless man. Note: he is so well known that the headline uses his actual name.

I could say much more about my parents, but in summary they are awesome.

Pre-baby, sometimes Mum and Dad visited. Mum talked (complained) about how crowded Brighton was and how much cups of tea and buttery slices of cake cost. Dad bought obscene quantities of cheese from Brighton's Cheese Cave and talked (complained) about parking issues.

My parents tentatively suggested that I might need help 'when the baby came', but I was sure this wouldn't be necessary.

'I've read *Parenting for Control Freaks*,' I explained. 'Everything will run to schedule. I know what I'm doing. I'm an adult now.'

Still, my parents insisted, wouldn't I at least want them around for the birth, just in case? Births aren't always straightforward. What if I ran out of cheese?

'Come if you like,' I said. 'But the birth WILL be very straightforward. I'm reading about hypnobirthing and I don't envisage any pain or difficulty.'

My parents visited Brighton soon after Lexi's birth and came straight to the hospital, excited to meet their new granddaughter.

My mum picked Lexi up, changed her and helped rock her to sleep.

Dad dumped a load of cheese on my lap, aka my C-section incision, and told me I looked ill and needed more dairy.

I decided that Dad should drive me home while Demi stocked the house for our arrival.

I can't remember where Mum was.

(Demi: 'Your mum was cleaning our house from top to bottom. She is wonderful.')

Demi was instructed to buy *lots* of carbohydrates. I'd prepared many wholesome, healthy freezer meals, of course. Food to nourish us for the long months ahead. I hadn't considered that tired, hormonal women do not want nourishing food. They want chocolate and tubes of Pringles.

Demi seemed pretty relieved to be given early release from the hospital, having spent three days and nights on the overly warm maternity ward, sleeping on upright old-lady chairs. In fact, I think he may have skipped out of the ward.

'What are you going to do with the baby in the car?' Dad asked. 'Hold her on your lap?'

This innocent suggestion resulted in a lot of swearing on my part.

'Stupid, dangerous idea . . . safe CAR seat! . . . It's not the fucking 1970s . . .'

The midwife, overhearing this, said, 'You do have a proper car seat, don't you?'

'Of course I have a car seat,' I snapped. 'I worked out how to use the thing MONTHS ago.'

The midwife walked briskly away, probably resolving not to give me any of the free wet-wipe samples.

'I'll bring the car to the front of the hospital,' said Dad.

'That's where the ambulances pull up,' I said.

'It'll only be for a few minutes,' said Dad. 'It'll be *fine*.'

Ten minutes later, with Lexi in my arms, I staggered out of the hospital, grey-faced and wincing as my C-section incision tugged and pulled.

Dad waited outside by his car, beaming with pride at the arrival of his granddaughter, and blissfully unaware that three ambulances were behind him, flashing their lights and beeping their horns.

'Dad,' I said. 'You haven't fitted the car seat. You've just sat it in the back without strapping it down.'

'Oh, it's safe enough,' he said with an airy wave of his hand. 'They didn't even *have* car seats when you were born.'

'How could this possibly be safe!' I exploded. 'If the car stops suddenly, the seat will fly forwards.'

Behind us, an ambulance gave a loud beep.

'Well, I don't know how to fit the seat,' Dad snapped. 'You'll have to do it.'

I'd practised fitting a baby car seat. I had not practised fitting a car seat with a C-section incision while holding a newborn baby and hearing three ambulances beeping their horns.

Perhaps I didn't need to swear at Dad so much. But *honestly*, I was *not* being 'obsessive'.

Back home, Mum had cleaned and tidied our whole house (thanks, Mum). The fridge was stocked with mountains of cheese (thanks, Dad). Demi had bought lots of crisps and cake and made me a cup of tea (thanks, Demi).

Once inside, Demi and I showed our lovely little baby daughter our home, believing her to be far more cognitive than she was, in that idiotic way first-time parents do.

Lexi cried.

I felt a worried pang in my chest.

What should I do? There was no midwife to ask.

It occurred to me that I had absolutely no experience with babies. No little brothers or sisters. No nieces or nephews. Nothing.

I grew up with a twin sister who, as twins tend to be, was exactly my age. When I was a baby, she was a baby, and I certainly wasn't qualified to do any sibling childcare at the time.

My sister hadn't had kids yet and was similarly ignorant about newborns.

It dawned on me that Lexi was the first baby I'd ever held.

And come to think of it, I wasn't really a baby person.

My parents tried to give helpful (useless) advice, the brunt of which being, 'It's a long, hard, horrible job and you'll just have to get used to it. Stick the baby in the bedroom, close the door and walk away.'

My parents, as mentioned previously, brought up twins in the 1970s. Their child-rearing philosophy was simple: 'Keep the baby alive.'

Any grander goals (sleep training, bathing, etc.) would risk exhaustion.

I, on the other hand, had a baby sleep schedule to put in place. If this didn't happen, I was certain the world would crumble.

Unaccustomed to needing help, I took on the role of angry dictator. When my parents asked what they could do, I gave vague, fatigue-gnawed instructions, then barked at them for not reading my mind and getting things *exactly* right.

My parents were very kind when I shouted that they were overstimulating Lexi with their chatter. They never once told me to stop being so horrible and ungrateful. They were just happy to help, and I think they understood I was struggling with a lot more than just a baby.

My whole life had changed.

I oscillated between snappy, irritable, 'I can do it, I'm fine, it was only a C-section,' to wailing, 'I can't cope. *Why* is she crying again? My stitches hurt. I need emergency chocolate. This baby absolutely *isn't* telling me what it needs.'

I've always been a 'can do' person – someone who mucks in and doesn't cause problems. The sort who walks home with heavy shopping bags cutting their hands rather than accepting someone's offer to drive five minutes out of their way.

'Really, the bags aren't that heavy. Just a few kilos of potatoes, twelve cans of Guinness, a couple of solid gold bars and some lead . . . it's *fine*.'

I got emotional on my wedding day when so many people travelled 'just for me'.

Needing help from others, asking for advice, leaning on people . . . it was hard. I felt so selfish. Plus, other people weren't doing it right.

My parents stayed with us for a week. Then, they selfishly abandoned us. When they headed back home, all the safety nets were gone.

We would have to survive with this baby by ourselves. Do our own washing-up. Buy our own cheese.

After one day on our own, I began to panic.

'Lexi isn't telling us what she needs,' I told Demi. 'I strongly suspect we're getting it all wrong, misinterpreting Lexi's cries, not giving her what she needs and consequently making her cry more.'

I began obsessively re-reading baby books, searching for answers to my many, many questions.

It was all very well to schedule feeds, sleeps, etc. but not one book indicated how these things could be achieved.

Lexi seemed to need feeding every hour and then she'd sleep for ages – only to wake up at the most inconvenient times like 3 a.m. or right in the middle of *The Real Housewives of Orange County*.

'What are we going to do?' I asked Demi. 'We need to make this sleep schedule work or I'll go mad. I can't do random.'

'Why don't we work out when Lexi feeds and sleeps, and see if there's a pattern?' Demi suggested. 'That way, we can maybe work out something with the breast pump.'

This seemed like a good idea.

We would monitor and record Lexi's habits, much as a naturalist (not the naked people – the wildlife people) studies animals and comes to definite conclusions about their habits and needs.

We created an Excel spread sheet. Yes, we really did that. The spread sheet recorded Lexi's feeds, sleeps and toilet habits, with a helpful space for notes.

After a few days, the notes were fuller than any of the tick boxes – many of which I couldn't tick with any real certainty.

'Fed?? Seemed to feed for three minutes, then she stopped. Does this count as a feed?'

'Slept?? Think she may have fallen asleep on my shoulder for a few seconds, but when I laid her down she woke up.'

There was a further problem – a lot of the time I failed to recall what had happened five or ten minutes previously.

Hormones, morphine and tiredness conspired to make me a slack-jawed simpleton.

I couldn't tell you what day it was, let alone fill in tick boxes with any accuracy.

Demi filled in the sheet as best he could, but really it only gave us one tangible fact: babies are random. Totally, utterly random. Especially in the pooing and weeing department – it's unpredictable, and we have the Excel spread sheet to prove it.

We resorted to Plan C: obsessive Google searching.

Why wasn't our baby feeding every four hours like the other sleep-scheduled babies? Was there someone who could come in and 'fix' our baby?

After searching terms like 'baby feeding nightmare', 'erratic feeding baby' and 'rebel baby', we discovered that random feeding patterns do have a name – 'cluster feeding'. In this case, cluster wasn't a good thing. Not like those nice clusters of nuts in granola.

Some babies are more random than others. Ours was one of them.

Lexi fed every hour or so, then took a nice long six-hour nap right in the middle of the day, giving her energy to torture us during the cold, dark, wintery nights.

Cluster feeding sounded like bad news. But if something had a name, it could be fixed. Right?

Acceptance wasn't OK.

We needed a nice scientific solution.

We didn't find it.

In fact, quite the opposite. Science was at odds with the random world of babies.

The breast pump, which should have been a simple 'extract milk and feed in millimetres' concept, sometimes extracted half a pint, sometimes nothing at all – there was no rhyme or reason to it.

The sleep app that made hairdryer noises sometimes worked, sometimes didn't. You could never tell whether to bother with it.

(Demi: 'I also remember making a recording of the tap running. That worked a few times, then Lexi got wise to it.')

And all that feeding . . . how much was Lexi getting out exactly? Too much? Not enough? Who really knew?

Nothing in this brave new world could be measured or quantified.

I watched lovely, soft-faced, smiling mothers at baby groups – you know, the naturally nurturing ones. The ones who want nothing more in life than babies. Who probably worked in a nursery at some point. Who grew up with baby brothers and sisters and a Tiny Tears doll.

I'd watch those women and think, 'You're wonderful. The world needs more of you. But I find all this baby stuff tremendously confusing. Yes, yes – of course I love my baby. But enjoy? Not so much right now.'

In fact, I felt very, very sad and trapped. And tired. So, so tired.

'My boobs *hurt* and nothing can fix it. I need to *sleep* at night. And our baby isn't doing what *other* babies do,' I'd complain.

'What about seeing a midwife?' Demi would suggest. 'Or the doctor?'

'What can they do? If all those baby books won't give us answers, how can they? All they'll tell us is "Baby will lead the way, your baby will tell you what it needs."'

'They might—'

'No, they *can't*. No one can fix this. I shall be uncomfortable and tired forever. Lexi's very cute, but let's face it: we're not baby people and we've ruined our lives.'

Our shiny new baby, although lovely, was clearly broken. We had it so much worse than anyone else in the *world*.

My sister, who was studying a nutrition course, suggested I take vitamins to ease my mental hormones.

'I don't have time for that!' I raged. 'Don't you understand how much work this is? I'm trying to figure out something totally random!'

'It's just one pill. I'll buy them for you. All you need to do is—'

'No, no, no. You don't understand. I wake up, I feed the baby. I try to get the baby to sleep. She won't sleep. Then she wakes up all night. I'm confused. There's no time for vitamins.'

'It's really only a few minutes—'

'I'll forget.'

'But I could set an alarm.'

'An alarm could wake the baby! How could you suggest such an insensitive thing?'

I was a Negative Nellie. A Debbie Downer. A Stressy Bessie.

(Demi: 'You weren't that bad. It was a very tough time and you were doing the brunt of the work. I thought you coped very well.')

Maybe it was hormones. But also I'm pretty sure I was quite rationally upset because my previous fun self had been shat all over by Mother Nature (that bitch).

Where had my life gone?

I was home almost all the time. There were no trips to quirky cabaret waffle restaurants. No paddleboard experiments on Brighton beach. No fun day trips to cider festivals. My greatest adventure was a dash to Tesco for wet wipes, clinging on to my sore boobs on the way.

I now know that all those clichés ('This will pass', 'You'll learn to love it', 'They'll be at school before you know it', blah blah blah) turn out to be true, but I didn't know that then. I thought there was something wrong with me and I was destined for a life of misery.

Other mothers didn't seem as trapped or unhappy as me. Some of them even smiled when I spoke to them at baby weigh-ins. They were coping. More than coping – it looked very much like they were *enjoying* motherhood. How, if they weren't drinking beer, eating sushi and going on Brighton Pier roller coasters? What on earth was left?

I phoned my mum to complain, dressed up as, 'Oh, I just phoned for a chat.'

'Your social life moves to your home when you have kids,' Mum advised. 'Why not invite some other mums over?'

'I'm at home too much already,' I moaned. 'The last thing I want to do is spend more time looking at our swirly, brown carpet and crap storage heaters. We can't have people round our house. We barely fit in it ourselves. There's only one small sofa. I'm not sitting on the floor – I have breastfeeding backache. And you can't make guests sit on the floor. It's rude.'

'Well, you could always move to a new place,' Mum suggested. 'Somewhere bigger. A bit more suitable for a family.'

'In the city?' I shrieked. 'Bigger than a one-bedroom flat? We're not millionaires.'

'What about moving out of Brighton, then?' said Mum. 'Move nearer your dad and me. We'll help you out.'

But I didn't want to move into a 'family area' back then.

I just wanted my old life back.

#11 LIE – BABY BLUES ONLY LAST A FEW DAYS

Lexi was born in November, which is usually a fun time of year. Fireworks night. Christmas on the way. Starbucks sell those frou-frou 'white-chocolate, Christmas-cake, gingersnap'-flavoured lattes. Twinkly lights go up around the Brighton clock tower.

Lexi *was* lovely. Aww . . . her little head, hands, etc. However, life at home with a newborn baby was still a little bit shit.

First off, I was having something of an ego crisis. I'd gone from doing a job I was reasonably good at (depending on which reviews you read) to one I was totally not suited to. I had zero experience of motherhood but some idiot had OK'd my job interview and given me a security pass to Baby Towers. Now I was failing miserably. Well, no wonder! I wasn't qualified.

According to the midwife, I had baby blues.

When I told Demi this, he tried his best to make everything cheerful. He surprised me with aforementioned frou-frou flavoured lattes from Starbucks, sent me funny text messages and delivered glasses of water and cups of tea to wherever I happened to be sitting. He told me if he could borrow my boobs and do the breastfeeding he would, and sympathised hugely with the unfairness of it all – the fact I had to do most of the work when he was clearly the most nurturing of the two of us.

When the midwife came for the first 'let's make sure you're not failing your baby horribly' home check, we talked more about baby blues.

'I'm not really a baby person,' I confessed. 'So I don't expect to feel particularly happy about all this. But that's rational, isn't it? My life has just been snatched away. I'm going to feel a bit low about that. There's no need to label me. Only god can judge.'

'Do you feel anxious?' the midwife asked.

'Of course I feel anxious. I'm woken up at all hours of the night, never knowing when I'll grab my next bit of sleep, while simultaneously ensuring the survival of a delicate infant.'

'What about sad?'

'Yes. I cried this morning because we'd run out of hot chocolate.'

'Baby blues,' the midwife diagnosed. 'Don't worry. It will pass.'

'When?'

'Usually within the first few days, but everyone is different.'

I hate those sorts of answers.

What a cop-out.

I waited for the freaky emotional stuff to pass, but a month came and went and I was still crying over nonsense.

As we rolled towards our first 'baby' Christmas, I was fully strapped in to the hormonal roller coaster. Up and down we go! One minute, laughing and dancing around the kitchen. The next, crying, tired, fed up and anxious. Oh, so anxious.

Pre-baby, I thought 'baby blues' just meant a few emotional days needing more hugs. Possibly accompanied by a tiny cry, softened by the love and happiness of being a parent. But my 'baby blues' lasted for months.

Apparently, months of 'baby blues' is normal. It's one of the many things midwives and other mothers are too 'kind' to tell you before you have children. Like vaginal tearing, contractions that feel like acid being vomited into your insides, and life-long 'little bit of wee coming out' incontinence.

People think it's nicer not to say.

Possibly there is a survival-of-the-species element here too, because if people told you the full story (you won't have a lie-in for at least ten years; your car will *always* be an unhygienic nightmare; you won't be able to leave the house without packing a load of stuff and/or shouting at people) no one would have children.

Was my complaining and manic anxiety due to hormones or to my old life having been ripped away and replaced with pain and confusion?

Probably both.

Either way, I had this feeling of dread in my body quite a lot of the time during the newborn stage. A lethal cocktail of hormone changes, exhaustion and sore boobs left me feeling worried, manic and weepy morning, noon and night.

I'd never been depressed before. I wouldn't recommend it – it's horrible.

Yes, there was the occasional respite. When *I'm a Celebrity Get Me Out of Here* was on and Lexi was asleep. Or Demi was forcing me to do the conga around the kitchen. But mainly, I was either anxious or overwhelmed.

I know now that those feelings don't last. They pass. They PASS! But when you're in it, it doesn't feel that way. Especially when you're told baby blues only last a few days.

FYI, if you've just had a baby and are possibly suffering a few baby blues and thinking, 'Whoa, this shit is bringing me down, man!' I promise I grow and transform in this book, and that life is now super-sparkly-rainbow awesome. There *is* a happy ending.

I love having a family now. But in the early days . . . well, there's a lot to deal with.

Pre-baby, I 'managed' bad days by having an all-night drinking session, followed by a day feeling so ill that I could only focus on my hangover.

I definitely couldn't do that now.

So I had two choices. I could learn to handle my feelings, to sit with the sadness and anxiety, to nurture myself, to understand and accept and wait patiently for this time to pass. Or I could distract myself by eating stuff, buying stuff, watching TV and squashing my feelings into an unhealthy little ball that would certainly explode later.

I chose the latter.

Because I couldn't use alcohol to mentally obliterate myself, I opted for the next-best legal mood-altering substance – chocolate.

Apparently, chocolate has some kind of natural antidepressant in it. I didn't know that at the time. All I knew was that most commercial hot chocolates were in no way strong enough. Some hot chocolate was almost the same colour as *milk*, for goodness' sake. Who let that insipid low-cocoa blend out of the door?

Wherever I went, I demanded industrial-strength cacao. If the drink wasn't the same colour as a 70 per cent cocoa Green & Black's bar, I sent it back in outrage.

At Costa, I would explain at length to the barista how I needed *at least* six scoops of cocoa. Yes, six. And don't look at me that way. As I told that midwife, only god can judge.

Starbucks was right out, since they use syrup to make their hot chocolate, which is ridiculously low in cocoa content. It was a bad day if *anyone* suggested Starbucks for a coffee break.

During this cocoa frenzy, I discovered a stupidly strong hot-chocolate brand in our local supermarket. It was called something like 'King Cacao' and boasted warning labels about overconsumption.

A month into my baby-blues cocoa addiction, the local supermarket stopped stocking this product, citing low demand.

This sent me into both wild panic and blind fury.

WHY would they stop stocking King Cacao? I was buying three tubs a week – clearly it was in demand!

I asked to see the manager, who (frightened by my wild-eyed ranting) promised to reorder but told me this *might* take a few days.

A few days! This was *outrageous*!

It began to dawn on me that I may have a problem. Could chocolate be addictive? People talk about chocolate addiction, but always in a jokey way.

'Ho, ho, I'm a chocoholic!' people say if pressed about bad habits. 'I couldn't live without my chocolate fix!'

But my habit didn't seem all that funny.

I decided I'd better do the sensible thing. No, not seek medical advice. Take an internet addiction quiz.

The first question was: *'Can you get through a week without your substance?'*

A week! Of course I can't get through a week. Clearly, after my panicked reaction to that supermarket stock issue, a *day* without my substance was too long.

The next question was: *'Have you ever used drugs at higher doses than recommended or needed?'*

Quadruple-heaped-teaspoon hot chocolates with a sprinkling of cocoa on top?

Yes.

On to the next question: *'Have you ever neglected your family because of drug use?'*

There was a time when I delayed changing Lexi by twenty minutes because I had to go to the supermarket to stock up on hot chocolate and semi-skimmed milk. So, technically, yes.

'Has drug use ever created problems between you and your partner?'

Definitely yes. I was forever asking Demi to go out and get hot-chocolate powder, not to mention using all the milk and leaving him without milk for his tea.

Demi asked why I couldn't leave just a bit of milk, a few teaspoons for his tea. But he didn't understand – that would be a precious few teaspoons' less hot chocolate. And I needed that hot chocolate.

I answered a few more questions like 'Can you stop your drug use?' (I have no intention of finding out right now, and don't ask me that again), and about using multiple drugs at once (yes – hot chocolate and paracetamol) and withdrawal symptoms (no idea, but if I ever stop I'll let you know).

I was starting to worry at this point. Maybe I should see a doctor. Get some counselling. Fortunately, the next questions made me feel better: *'Have you ever lost a job because of drug use?'*

I don't have a job right now, ha ha ha! I am taking time off from work to be a boring mother, crying at home over her hot chocolate. Take THAT, drug survey! No one can sack me.

'Have you ever been arrested for drug use?'

No. I barely even shouted at that supermarket manager. It was not verbal abuse and no police were called.

'Do you ever have flashbacks due to drug use?'

Nope.

Things were looking up now.

'Have you ever gotten into fights when under the influence of drugs?'

Are we counting verbal fights with Demi? When I steal the Double Decker he's hidden in the wine rack or eat the 'They're for Christmas Day' After Eights?

Are we counting being angry at Costa baristas when they don't follow my clearly articulated instructions and instead serve me milky, weak hot chocolate with paltry cocoa content?

No, they must mean physical fights.

No, then.

By now, I was beginning to suspect the quiz wasn't designed with chocolate addicts in mind, which further reassured me that chocolate couldn't possibly be addictive.

Cheered by this good news, I ordered pure cacao powder from the internet and proceeded to make my own extra-strong home blend while I waited for the local supermarket to restock my beloved King Cacao.

Consume, consume, consume – that's how I coped with all those anxious, sad, difficult feelings in the beginning.

I drank shedloads of hot chocolate (as outlined), ordered baby gadgets galore and ploughed through whole tins of Christmas cookies.

They say the first stage of grief is denial. And I was grieving. Clearly. Because I kept crying all the time.

Home from hospital with a big pile of carbs. I'm smiling (who wouldn't be with so much yellow food!) but crying inside.

PART II: CHANGE OR DIE. THERE IS NO THIRD OPTION

#12 LIE – YOUR POST-BABY BELLY GOES BACK TO NORMAL AFTER SIX WEEKS

On Christmas Day, after the Christmas Eve From Hell mentioned at the beginning of the book, my mum and dad came to visit. I raged at them because I was sleep-deprived and fed up. Then I raged at everyone for drinking champagne at 11 a.m. I was breastfeeding and couldn't have alcohol, after all. This was very insensitive.

> *(Demi: 'I didn't drink anything on Christmas Day, even though there were six bottles of Guinness Original in the cupboard. I am outraged that you can't remember this act of heroism.')*

It was a shit Christmas Day, made even more shit by the fact that my Christmas onesie wouldn't zip up around the middle because I was still so elaborately stretched out and saggy.

As I wrestled with the many losses of motherhood, one of the big things to grieve was the loss of my former body.

It wasn't what it used to be and showed no signs of returning to normal.

I waited patiently for the six-week marker – when my womb would, allegedly, shrink to the size of a fist and I would no longer look pregnant.

Six weeks came and went, and I still looked noticeably with-child.

Also, I needed special pants to hold in my weird, stretched stomach skin. I was back and forth to the doctors with mastitis, headaches, a weird lump on my knee, etc. every five minutes and I regularly napped with my mouth slightly open.

Not only had I lost my freedom, I'd also lost the youthful body I'd once known.

I assumed my figure would return once my C-section wound healed, but as the weeks progressed nothing much was changing. My body was not 'snapping back' into shape, like all those Hollywood bikini celebrities you see in glossy magazines. In fact, it hadn't 'snapped' at all. No – the word was 'sagged'.

My entire midsection, boobs included, was now deflated like a week-old party balloon. My boobs were pretty ginormous due to breast-feeding, but they were still clearly a good inch lower now. And my stomach – it looked like a wrinkly paper bag. A full one.

Also, the following elderly-person symptoms – things I had assumed were temporary and associated with the C-section – now seemed to be permanent:

- Irritable bowel (farting unexpectedly, to give it the non-medical term)
- Mild incontinence (weeing unexpectedly)
- Haemorrhoids (anus inside-outus, to use the Latin)
- Indigestion (chocolate and fried stuff make burny throat!)

- Varicose veins
- Rampant mole growth
- Saggy skin (and boobs)
- SLOOOWW metabolism (get fat quicky-quick!)
- Loss of physical strength, leaving me pathetically struggling to push a bed a few inches from the wall to pick up that KitKat I'd dropped down there

Not so long ago, I'd been a healthy(ish, if you don't count alcohol units) adult in my late twenties. Suddenly, I had rocketed into old age. I was a slow, staggering, farty, fat cow, crying and drinking hot chocolate all day long.

An internal battle raged.

I didn't want to be this person. This slow, incompetent, sick person. But my body didn't seem to be returning to normal any time soon. Wearing anything other than oversized Primark sweatshirts, leggings and jimmy jams was out of the question.

Ugh.

I desperately wanted *me* back. My former, youthful, physical body. The one that worked without all these bowel problems and that fitted regular clothing.

Christmas Day really should have been OK. Demi cooked the dinner, which from memory was chicken *(Demi – 'Beef!')*, and Mum was amazing, clearing everything up and helping get Lexi to sleep. We played some party games, which included a limbo challenge and a made-up game called 'rolly ball'.

It should have been fun, but I felt fat, old and fed up. I kept needing 'little naps' and went to bed at 9 p.m.

This was what I had to look forward to? Early nights and no booze while everyone else enjoyed themselves?

It turns out that, yes, that was exactly what I had to look forward to. But back then I didn't believe I'd learn to love it.

#13 LIE – NEWBORNS SLEEP ALL THE TIME

'How are you sleeping?'

People always ask new parents this, usually with sad, sympathetic eyes that say, 'I feel your pain.'

After Christmas and a very unremarkable 'Let's go to bed at 10 p.m.' New Year, Demi and I still weren't sleeping well. Lexi was nearing the magical milestone of three months – an age we'd been told was synonymous with 'sleeping through the night'.

However, this wasn't even close to happening. I was lucky if I grabbed three hours of uninterrupted sleep, and once I'd been woken up I found it very hard to drop back off again.

Lack of sleep sometimes brought on hallucinations, which weren't fun. Except for the evening I saw little toy racing cars driving around the toilet seat. That actually was quite fun.

As the New Year began, I decided to have one last crack at 'baby sleep training'.

New Year, new start and all of that.

If other people had done sleep training, surely I could too. *Surely.*

Just as soon as I stopped crying.

One cold, January morning, I took yet another look at the baby sleep-training schedule, still handily taped behind the baby's wardrobe door.

'It's 7 a.m. now,' I told Demi. 'Lexi's just fed. No matter what happens, we can't feed her again until 11 a.m.'

Half an hour later, Lexi cried again. A lot. Clearly she was desperately hungry. Possibly skirting malnutrition.

I skimmed through the baby sleep-training books, but there were no instructions on what to do if a baby seemed hungry at non-scheduled feeding times.

I decided to feed Lexi, just in case, and hope she'd go a bit longer next time.

Half an hour later, Lexi cried again. A lot. Soon it became screaming. She must still be hungry. Maybe she didn't get enough out last time.

I fed her again. Then Lexi fell asleep for six hours.

'Should we wake her up?' I asked Demi four hours in. 'The schedule says she's due another feed right now.'

We whispered Lexi's name in an effort to rouse her, but she wasn't having any of it.

'What should we do?' I asked Demi. 'How do you wake babies? Sing them Metallica songs? Dunk them in cold water?'

But these things seemed cruel.

All the sleep-training books were extremely vague about how to wake babies. The only suggestion I read was a fairly useless: 'Wake baby if asleep.'

So what now?

'We need someone who understands babies,' said Demi. 'I'll call the local midwife and see what she advises.'

Ten minutes later, Demi returned with bad news.

'The midwife says we shouldn't do a schedule,' he said. 'We should let the baby lead the way and feed when she wants to feed. It's called "on-demand" feeding and the midwife says it's the best, most natural way. She says babies naturally start sleeping through the night at three months. We should just wait.'

'But what about my sore boobs?' I said. 'And my anxiety? And my lack of sleep? And those teeny-tiny racing cars I saw rushing around the toilet seat last night?'

'She said you'll just have to get used to it.'

After a little cry, I tried to accept my fate: carry on feeding Lexi whenever she wants to be fed; ignore the schedule idea; go slowly mad through lack of sleep.

Could boobs fall off through painful overuse? Could that happen? I assumed not, but who really knew?

'The midwife recommended a good book about on-demand feeding,' Demi continued. 'It's called something like *Breastfeeding is Magic and You Should Do It All Day Long*.'

'I hate that title.'

'Shall I get us a copy?'

'Yes, please.'

Demi borrowed a copy of *Breastfeeding is Magic and You Should Do It All Day Long* from the library, and I scoured its pages for survival tips and practical advice. There were none – only anecdotal stories from mothers who'd breastfed for years and loved it.

The book celebrated the magical properties of breast milk and the fact you can calm your baby instantly by shoving a boob in its mouth.

Breastfeeding is Magic and You Should Do It All Day Long was very against routine, assuring mothers that babies tell you when they need breast milk.

Sometimes, the book said, babies need breastfeeding three times an hour, all day and all night long. And this is fine. All perfectly normal.

A previous book borrower had underlined the word 'normal'. Obviously, her big concern was abnormality.

This was not my concern. I couldn't care less about being abnormal. I cared about sleeping at night and not being anxious.

Breastfeeding is Magic and You Should Do It All Day Long did have one suggestion for a better night's sleep – it recommended putting the baby in bed with you. This would make feeding easier, it said, and everyone would be more relaxed and happy.

Breastfeeding is Magic and You Should Do It All Day Long pointed out that parents all over the world sleep with their babies in the bed. It is very normal (that word again). To be fair, it does feel natural to sleep with babies in the bed. But lots of things are natural and also a bad idea. Relying on breastfeeding as contraception, for example. Or cleaning your teeth with twigs.

The book went on to compare a baby cot with bars to a prison – isolating a baby from its carers, depriving it of the loving warmth of its mother and potentially causing psychological meltdowns later in life.

Shit.

We'd been putting Lexi in a cot for months now.

I informed Demi that we were being very cruel and that a change in attitude was necessary.

Demi gave his tired assurances that my new demands would be met, with the patience of a man who knew these demands would probably change in a few hours.

As I bossed Demi around, Lexi started crying.

I followed the *Breastfeeding is Magic and You Should Do It All Day Long* advice and let Lexi feed for a minute, even though she'd only just fed.

It worked.

Lexi stopped crying.

This felt great. Just go with the flow, man! Magic boobs!

By the end of the day, my boobs were sorer than ever. I mean, agonisingly sore. Being used as a human pacifier was taking its toll.

Also, our household was out of tea, eggs and hot-chocolate powder, since the 'stick a boob in your baby's mouth every time she cries' approach meant I couldn't go to the supermarket. It was bitterly cold

Suzy K Quinn

outside and there was no way I was sitting on some freezing garden wall, whacking my poor, goosebumpy bare skin out to breastfeed.

Night-time came – and ended up being the worst night's sleep I had ever had.

Lexi fed voraciously. Every hour, pretty much. And she seemed really unsettled, pulling her knees to her chest as if her tummy hurt.

I followed the *Breastfeeding is Magic and You Should Do It All Day Long* advice and put Lexi in bed beside me so she could just 'roll on to the feed' whenever she liked, but this made my own sleep impossible.

Every muscle in my body was tense as I worried that I'd crush little Lexi in my sleep. I opened my eyes at every noise – and babies make a lot of noises.

Three days of 'on-demand' feeding resulted in eye-wateringly sore boobs and eye-twitching, manic tiredness. It was a great technique for turning a normal(ish) woman into a psychopath.

Reality began to dawn on me: I was not an easy-going, go-with-the-flow baby mama. I just wasn't. Maybe this wouldn't work for me.

Tired and brain dead, I delved further into *Breastfeeding is Magic and You Should Do it All Day Long* for further advice and possible phone numbers for psychiatric therapists.

I found anecdotal stories of mothers who'd been breastfeeding on demand for three years or more. Some mothers had been doing on-demand feeding for five years and turfed their partner out of the bed to accommodate the all-day, all-night feedathon.

FIVE YEARS of interrupted sleep!

No fucking way was I giving up five years of my life or kicking Demi out of bed. Lexi would be lucky to get six months of breastfeeding out of me. If that.

After many crying fits (mine), I decided there must be another way. If the schedule didn't work and the on-demand approach was awful, surely there was a middle ground? An app, perhaps?

78

I studied every book I could get my hands on, between manic Google searches.

Other people had done this baby stuff. Other people like me – obsessive, anxious, controlling people.

Surely someone had the answer?

Lexi, wide awake as usual. The little tinker.

#14 LIE - SLEEP WHEN THE BABY SLEEPS

In the depth of my baby confusion and misery, I did what any sensible person would do.

I complained a lot on Facebook.

Of course, I dressed up the complaining with beautiful new-baby pictures. I'd post a cute picture of Lexi, then write something like, 'This innocent little face kept me up all night, ha ha ha! AGAIN! Ha ha ha. IT'S BEEN MONTHS NOW. WHY WON'T SHE GIVE IT A REST?'

'Sleep when the baby sleeps,' people replied. 'Then you'll get enough rest.'

Sleep when the baby sleeps?

Impossible.

I'd tried many times to sleep in the daytime, my heart pounding with anxiety as I wondered just when my boob services would be called upon.

Would Lexi cry in half an hour? An hour? Three hours? Not knowing was stressful and stress is the enemy of sleep.

Many a time, I'd lie in a sunlit room, my eyes squeezed closed and willing myself to fall asleep, knowing full well I was exhausted and badly needed rest. But telling yourself, 'GO TO SLEEP! SLEEP NOW! QUICK – BEFORE THE BABY WAKES UP' doesn't work. So I just stayed awake and complained on Facebook.

One of my friends, Big Gay Rob, suggested trying semi-scheduled feeding. It was quite the thing these days, he said. A moderate middle ground. None of this 'all or nothing' stuff. Don't be a slave to your baby, but don't totally ignore its cries either.

I was sceptical. After all, I'd read so many baby books and heard so much 'good advice'. None of it was working. It was all awful! Nothing was fixing our broken baby. Nothing!

I was also dubious about Big Gay Rob's ability to give baby advice. He didn't have kids and didn't want kids. In fact, I'd never seen him anywhere that would be suitable for children. As a handsome gay about town, his natural habitat was a bar or club.

But it turned out Big Gay Rob had helped out a lot with his baby sister and knew a thing or two about parenting. Probably more than we did, actually. It's surprising what hidden talents your friends have, isn't it?

The advice on semi-scheduled feeding went something like this: 'Most babies don't know how to sleep, so the first step is teaching them how to sleep.'

This was sort of a revelation. The missing piece in the baby sleep-training puzzle.

Teach Lexi how to fall asleep? I thought sleeping was a natural thing. If a baby was tired, she would drop off. Right?

Apparently not. Apparently, babies often cry when they're tired. But confused, sleep-deprived mothers often confuse this with hunger (or just want to shove anything in their baby's mouth to shut it up while they cling to the last few moments of sleep before dawn).

Feeding babies when they're not hungry starts an overfeeding cycle, which gives the baby an upset tummy and an even more disturbed night. Babies who are overfed and overstimulated have trouble drifting off, work themselves into hour-long screaming fits and are very unsettled – waking regularly at night.

Whoa.

This was us! This described our baby exactly!

Fancy that. Newborns – along with being colour blind, incontinent and unable to stop attacking themselves with their own limbs – *don't even know* how to fall asleep!

It got more interesting.

Breastfeeding is a tremendous source of comfort for a baby, whether they're hungry or not. Once a baby is in the habit of overfeeding, they get too much 'fore milk', which is watery. This gives them wind and tummy ache and causes them to feed even more.

It's a vicious circle, apparently. Little feeds create wind. And wind creates a desire for more feeding to ease the pain as breast milk has a painkiller in it.

All this 'overfeeding' stuff was making a lot of sense. And teaching a baby how to sleep . . . this would explain why Lexi got all eye-twitchy, red-faced and screechy but didn't 'seem' tired.

I made myself a cup of non-caffeinated tea (caffeine goes into breast milk and causes wakefulness), held a sleeping Lexi on my lap and proceeded to learn all about semi-scheduled 'moderate mother' feeding, via the weblinks Rob sent me.

Of course, being tired and sleep-deprived, not much of the information sank in the first time around. But on the third look, I got the gist of it – how to escape our sleep torture prison.

When Demi came in from work, I told him the escape plan.

'We need to teach Lexi how to sleep,' I told him. 'Be all calm and laid-back and make the bedroom super-dark and cosy.'

We proceeded to make our bedroom VERY dark at night, and I mean WARTIME blackout. The kind of dark where you trip over the nappy-rash cream and swear at whichever idiot left it there (must be Demi – I don't live with anyone else. Oh no, wait, it was me . . .).

Yes, we were tired. We did not want to measure windows and hang new curtains. But we did it, and also pushed clothes into the big door gaps to shut out the light. And put cotton wool in the keyhole just to make *absolutely* sure.

Perhaps I was a little obsessive. But wars are never won by the half-hearted.

Following the semi-schedule feed advice, night-time now began at the same time EVERY night, and EVERY night we brought Lexi into a dark room, fed her and put her in her cot.

This was similar to stricter sleep-training advice, but this time it worked because we worked really hard to make Lexi calm and keep her environment noise- and stimulation-free for a good hour before bedtime.

After three days or so, Lexi pretty much fell asleep within five minutes without any rocking or shushing. Then we became the envy of every parent on the block.

(Demi: 'Three days? It took a lot longer than that. But it's lovely you remember it happening so quickly. Your brain is a nice place.')

'Good god – you just put your baby down and she SLEEPS?' people would ask incredulously. 'No rocking? No shushing? No half-hour of walking her around, making Darth Vader breathing noises in her ear? This is a miracle! You have given birth to Christ himself!'

(Anyone offended by this statement – please note, my friend said this, not me. I do not believe I gave birth to Jesus Christ.)

The counterbalance to the night was a BRIGHT daytime. I became vigilant about this too. Perhaps a tiny bit crazy.

'NO! Don't close the curtains in the bedroom! This is NAP TIME, not NIGHT-TIME! No, I'm not being obsessive – we have a system!'

In the daytime, I woke Lexi up if she slept for longer than three hours. The internet gave some nice advice about this – stroke Lexi's hands and squeeze them gently. Yes, it did seem cruel picking up a sleeping baby, holding her under a bright light and singing 'Uptown Girl' at volume. But it's also cruel to sleep-torture people.

Sometimes, interfering elderly women would say things like, 'Never wake a sleeping baby!'

Doreen, Jean or Dot would be treated to a verbal tirade about bad sleep habits and how some people (me) couldn't cope with lack of sleep and ended up doing things like putting a duvet over their partner and hitting that duvet because the partner had been out for 'one' beer and ended up having three.

I would sum up this verbal ear-bashing by relaying the quote I'd pinned on my bathroom mirror: 'Babies need happy, well-rested mothers.'

There was a second part to the escape plan – tanking Lexi up in the daytime with breast milk.

In the daytime, I brought Lexi to me for feeding rather than waiting for her to cry. I did this every three hours or so. Sometimes a little earlier.

Semi-scheduled feeding is all about creating a relaxed, gentle routine, but it is also against overfeeding. The advice is not to breastfeed a baby more than every two and a half to three hours. Or four hours if you're formula-feeding, you lucky thing.

Semi-scheduled-feeding mothers recommended walking baby, jiggling baby or giving baby to someone else during the three-hour feeding break – just while everyone gets used to things.

This was great news.

Lexi's reign of boob terror was over.

I was taking charge.

Me!

In caveman times we lived in harmony with the sun and the moon and yes, we probably fed our babies whenever they cried. But we also didn't have hospitals or toilet paper. And I like both those things.

So feeding *approximately* every three hours, bringing Lexi to me rather than waiting for her cries, suited me just fine.

I *mustn't* whack my sore boobs out every ten minutes. *No.*

But similarly, I needn't worry about an exact schedule.

The moment I freed the Boob Two from baby prison, life started getting better.

I stopped feeling sore. I could leave the house much more regularly and plan trips. I slept for big stretches at night-time. I stopped slowly going insane. Those little toy cars racing around the toilet seat were a thing of the past.

Within a few weeks, Lexi sometimes slept from 10 p.m. to 7 a.m.

This felt pretty good.

Pain-free and getting a full night's sleep – what parent could ask for more?

Our old life back, perhaps?

Well, yeah. But that wasn't going to happen any time soon. Actually, it wasn't going to happen ever again. But I didn't know that then.

Two loves of my life: Demi with Lexi. He was always so calm with her. I absolutely was not. Please note – the tasteless Arsenal pillowcase was not my bedding choice.

#15 LIE – YOU'LL LOOK BACK ON THIS AS THE BEST TIME OF YOUR LIFE

When Lexi was three months old I received an invitation from some friends who lived in London. It was for one of those lovely, catch-up, reunion-type things. You know – we're all busy these days, but let's dedicate a little time to checking in and seeing where life has taken us. And having a few drinks while we're at it, ho ho ho!

London is an hour away from Brighton. The reunion-type thing was at 8 p.m.

For about three seconds, I considered it. Maybe I could shove Lexi in the pram, breastfeed her on the train and . . .

No.

It would be too exhausting. I just couldn't. Fancy hosting an event at 8 p.m. in the evening, anyway. That's bedtime.

Reality hit me like a Bumbo thrown across the room in a hormonal rage. Life had changed and the change wasn't temporary. I mean, it had been months already and I was still going to bed at old-lady time. The baby had not slotted into life and life wasn't going on as before.

Could it be that there would be no more nights out like we'd had before? That every evening from now on would be cut short – either because we needed to get back to the baby or because we needed a good night's sleep to endure the following day's onslaught?

Could it be that we would have to start enjoying different things? More wholesome activities like family walks in the woods and a nice roast dinner on a Sunday?

Could it be that I might actually look forward to a nice cup of tea and a buttery slice of cake, followed by a BBC crime drama and a nice early night?

God, I hoped not.

(Demi: 'Personally, I enjoyed little baby Lexi and loved this special time. You are a monster. However, I did feel really guilty about not being able to help. I know what you're going to say, Su. Guilt is a pointless emotion. But knowing that doesn't make it go away.')

Before I had Lexi, I assumed I'd still be able to have nights out. I'd just breast-pump some milk, stick it in the fridge and off I'd go.

I didn't realise Mother Nature would be very erratic in my case, never once giving me a consistent milk-pumping result. Add to that the fact I just didn't know how much milk Lexi was taking because I couldn't measure her stomach contents, and you get a tired new mother screeching: 'It's always me! It always has to be me. The breast pump doesn't work like that. I can't predict how much milk these boobs are going to pay out and anyway – I'm not getting up at 6 a.m. to breast-pump.'

I suddenly realised that this was for the long haul now – no days off, no sick leave, no holidays. Every day a little human being needed us for survival and we just had to be there. I mean, we wanted to be there, obviously. We were very invested in the survival of our baby. But we were also exhausted, sometimes ill, and in need of a break.

A few weeks later, the 'big night out' pictures appeared on Facebook. It was really nice, seeing all my friends having fun. I mentally inserted myself into the picture.

Who would I have been if I didn't have a young baby? The one giving the camera a happy thumbs-up? The one hilariously drinking wine straight from the bottle? The one holding a half-eaten, crescent-shaped poppadum over her mouth as a smile?

As I viewed these Facebook pictures, Lexi was sleeping on my giant stomach.

I was in a dressing gown. The T-shirt underneath was covered in boob milk. My eyebrows hadn't been plucked in a while and my hair probably needed cutting but who could say for certain? It had been in a ponytail since Lexi was born.

I did not fit into those Facebook pictures. I was not cut out for night-time public gatherings. Even if I'd been able to squeeze into nice clothes, I had breastfeeding backache that would make train travel on those thinly cushioned, itchy seats uncomfortable.

I was slowly realising that having a baby changes so much more than I'd ever imagined. It changes your body. It changes your lifestyle. And it also changes your friendships.

Kids do funny things to friendship. I don't mean they put on comedy glasses and squirt Silly String over it. I mean that my friendships changed when I had kids.

Pre-Lexi, I had many lovely, beautiful, special, kind and thoughtful friends. I assumed I'd still see lots of these friends when Lexi was born. Turns out, not so much. If their homes were devoid of parking or city-centre located or over three miles away then they may as well have lived on the moon. Plus, a lot of them were sleeping off hangovers during the daytime.

I loved these friends. I missed them terribly. But practical headaches put me off seeing them. It was a case of, 'I love you, but I love not having to travel anywhere with a screaming infant more.'

Friends offered to visit us, of course. But, as mentioned, our home was barely suitable for two adults and a baby, let alone guests. Not only did we lack guest furniture, but our house was also a mess of breast-pump equipment, baby clothes, swaddles and other less socially acceptable detritus like boob cream, nipple shields and abandoned bras. I was not going to put my friends through baby-detritus misery. Silly, really, because they wouldn't have minded. But hormones do ridiculous things to your thought processes.

Then there were friends who I should have kicked to the kerb a long time ago, but motherhood forced my hand.

Before kids, I was tolerant of people's flaws. I stumbled into friendships and knocked along with whoever seemed good fun. Most of the time I wasn't really sure how I met my friends. Probably in a pub somewhere. And I chose to see the best and ignore the worst.

Some of my friends drank way too much. It was fair to say they teetered on the tightrope of addiction. Others lost their temper too regularly or leaned on people quite a bit. Some were, if I'm being honest, quite messed-up emotionally. Even more than I was.

Pre-kids, it was all fine. We loved each other.

But when babies come along, things change.

Friends who aren't grown up enough to live a fully functioning adult life, who lack a clear route between their thoughts and emotions, who drink to the point of cross-eyed, shouty ranting – well, you don't have as much tolerance for that stuff when you have a baby.

When you're stressed and caring for a newborn, you don't have much to give.

I found my more self-centred friends naturally drifted away once I had a baby. I had nothing to give them. I was of no use, so they didn't bother with me, and I had no time or energy to bother with them. It was painful, realising how superficial these friendships had been, but really it was all for the best.

However, as some old friendships faded, so new ones grew.

There's that confusing phrase, isn't there? About God closing a door and opening a window? Or is it the other way around? (Either way, I've never really understood the window bit. Are we climbing through windows, is that it? Are we burglars now?)

Anyway.

When something ends, something else begins.

In this brave new world of parenthood, I made new friends who had kids. I hung out with my maternity gang and people I met at newborn-baby groups.

These people understood my confusion, pain and uncertainty because they were going through exactly what I was going through. Plus, they were geographically convenient and understood the need to meet in places that facilitated buggies and small children.

Babies are the great connectors, aren't they? They give us something in common with every other new parent on the planet.

Bit by bit, as my old life faded away, a new life grew.

I didn't want to lose my old friends, but I realised I needed extra friends to survive this new phase in our lives. People who knew my journey, pain and struggles. And actually wanted, rather than tolerated, a conversation about baby toilet habits.

The only people who fitted the bill at this time were other parents with newborns.

#16 LIE – IT'S JUST A PHASE

At least once a week, my lovely maternity gang would meet in one of the many 'not-very-child-friendly' Brighton cafes.

We'd head to Starbucks for a chat about modern parenting, while our babies screamed or tried to escape on to the busy street.

Starbucks hated us.

When I met up with my maternity gang, one of our favourite things to discuss was 'baby phases'.

A 'baby phase' is one of those casual terms used to dress up something unpleasant. (Like when you go to have your legs waxed and they say it will feel 'a bit tingly'. Or the nurse calls an injection a 'sharp scratch'.)

People say, 'it's *just* a phase' as if this somehow reduces the unpleasantness of your baby crying for two hours straight.

It doesn't.

In the baby world, phases are the random, odd things under-ones do that rarely feature in the baby books because they supposedly pass almost as soon as they come on.

Supposedly.

But mostly phases don't pass quickly. Which makes them not 'just a phase', but a long, miserable period of time.

Baby 'phases' for our gang included:

- Grunting at night (when your baby is technically sleeping, but worries you with their weird noises)
- Permanent runny nose
- Crying from 5 p.m. to 7 p.m. (aka the shitty hours)
- The 'why do they have a temperature for no reason?' phase
- And last but not least, the dreaded month of the mega poos

You can't talk about this stuff with friends who don't have kids. They don't understand or care. Nor are they a source of precious advice.

One of our maternity gang had her baby a month before the rest of us and was consequently a trailblazer and phase guru. Her son went through all the phases first, so she could tell us exactly what to look forward to.

During one of our Starbucks visits, Lexi hadn't pooed for a whole day.

This was greeted by big oohs and aahs from my maternity gang.

Trailblazing Tammy informed me that Lexi was entering the dreaded mega-poo phase.

She said, 'That's how the mega poos start. They don't go for ages and then it all comes out at once.'

I'm not going to go into graphic detail here, just in case you're eating. But I'll just throw out a few sentences:

- Clothes ruined.
- How could there be so much?
- Why does it always happen when we're not at home?
- I will ALWAYS remember to bring two sets of spare clothes . . .

As we were discussing the dreaded mega poos, Lexi went red-faced and filled her nappy.

I believe the phrase is 'uh-oh'.

Trailblazing Tammy put a sympathetic hand on mine. 'And it's *always* when you're out and about.'

'I'd better change her,' I said.

'Are you sure you're OK?' Trailblazing Tammy asked. 'You don't want an extra pack of wipes, just in case?'

But I thought I'd be fine. After all, Lexi was three months old now. I was an old pro. Whatever the size of the poo, I could handle an 'out and about' change. Right?

I had all the necessaries packed neatly in my bag AND I hadn't forgotten to restock today. In the parenting world, I was winning. It was all OK. Everything under control.

I calmly took Lexi to the overly warm Starbucks bathroom, which had one of those changing tables that fold out over the toilet.

All very civilised.

Once I started the change, I realised why Trailblazing Tammy had looked at me with such sympathy. This change was a horror story. We needed a full bath and total change of clothing. Possibly followed by the incineration of Lexi's current outfit.

Starbucks did not offer incineration facilities nor stock extra clothing.

I used every wet wipe I had to clean Lexi down. Then I dressed her in a new outfit and bagged up her old clothes – possibly for later incineration.

Then more mega poo came out. A lot more.

I always saw myself as someone who coped. Who got on with things. Who was never overwhelmed or out of her depth.

Well, when you have a screaming, naked child covered in excrement in a hot public toilet, solutions can seem very far away.

In my flustered state, I made the only choice possible – throw away the second set of clothes and bring Lexi out naked.

It was winter. Not the time of year for scantily dressed babies.

When I emerged from the bathroom, red-faced and with a naked, crying baby in my arms, I felt the eyes of the coffee shop upon me.

I imagine myself looking like a cartoon character after a bomb has gone off. You know, hair two feet high, eyes wide with shock.

'Are you OK?' my maternity friends asked, their eyes full of concern. 'Would you like some spare clothes?'

They proffered clean, folded and ironed changes of clothes, tucked neatly in their organised baby bags.

They were (still are) lovely mums.

I gratefully accepted a little sailor outfit and learned one of many, many lessons: always bring two sets of spare clothes.

As they say in survival situations, two is one and one is none.

Through each baby phase, Demi and I staggered along with the misguided hope that when *this* phase was over, things would be better. But in reality, with each new phase our apartment felt smaller and smaller due to the huge piles of baby-phase *stuff* we wasted our money on.

Having lived in a city for years, Demi and I were consumers. Our lives centred around buying shit.

Freshly baked, all-butter croissant from the French patisserie? Don't mind if I do. Signature cocktail with real juniper berries? Oh, go on then. Going gluten-free? Yes, I will enjoy the specialist organic supermarket for my paleo-cereal needs. My goodness, what a lot of choice!

(Demi: 'I have no idea what paleo cereal is and never liked all that gluten-free stuff you kept trying to force upon our household.')

In the city, all your consumerist desires can come true. The best restaurants, the most exciting and unusual foods and the newest entertainment. There was always something buzzy and exciting going on in Brighton city too: some guy juggling teddy bears just for the fun of it or bouncing to work on giant kangaroo boots (look them up, they're hilarious).

You could have a beer on a street balcony, listen to tribal-drum music or eat fresh prawns with buttered brown bread on the stony beach.

Fantastic.

However, we weren't bothering with city stuff now we had a young baby. I counted it as a good day if I made it down to the supermarket for wet wipes.

So consumerism took a new turn.

I started buying mail-order baby gadgets – things that would supposedly make these wretched phases easier.

We should have been growing up, of course. We should have realised that buying shit would not solve our problems and that a more profound mental shift was needed. Living in the moment. Accepting this new life. Letting go of the past, etc.

But we did not realise this.

Instead, with every new discomfort that occurred, I looked for a product to solve it.

As naive and desperate new parents, we were an advertiser's dream. I was more than willing to believe products could and would sidestep the many agonies of parenthood.

Take teething, for example.

At four months, Lexi started dribbling, banging her head on things, chewing inappropriate items like beer bottles, and sometimes (but not too often) waking up at night.

There I was, thinking life was getting easier, when Mother Nature grabbed a handful of shit and threw it at us.

Again.

BOOM! Dribbly, chewy, cranky baby, jerking awake in the small hours.

This seemed unfair. And may I add, what a terrible design, Mother Nature.

What could fix this problem? Surely someone had invented a product?

In my immaturity and naivety, I believed there must be some gadget or gizmo that could make things better.

I threw myself into internet research. Happily, there were plenty of shiny products on sale, complete with pictures of contented, smiling babies. Hooray! It was just as I thought. All I had to do was pay some money and soon contentment would be mine.

Great news.

How much do you want? Spare change for a hundred?

However, on closer inspection (Amazon reviews), it seemed some of these magical products might not actually work.

The amber teething necklace, for example, that claimed to leach out a 'gentle acid' against the baby's skin had no measurable, scientific proof of effectiveness. It was all guesswork.

Can baby say 'hooey'?

Teething granules sounded a little more plausible. Rubbing something into a baby's gums seemed like an actual medical thing.

I bought eight little sachets of granules for £5 plus postage.

The instructions said to use 'up to' eight sachets a day, depending on teething pain.

Essentially, I'd bought a single day's worth of teething relief at great expense.

Still. Worth a try.

The teething granules seemed to distract Lexi from her discomfort, in the same way playing a very, very loud song might temporarily stop her crying.

Lexi seemed curious as I shoved the granules into her mouth. And a little bit annoyed.

'What's this shit, then?' she seemed to be saying. 'Where's the milk?'

I waited for the miraculous calming effects to occur.

They didn't.

Lexi still dribbled and cried and chewed beer bottles, and she still woke up at night in pain, just the same as before.

I scoured the teething-granule packet for more instructions and discovered the active ingredient was something called Chamomilla, which is another word for camomile. Essentially, I was giving Lexi a cup of camomile tea. Not the hard-hitting painkiller I imagined.

Unperturbed, I bought gel-filled cold teething rings. When they arrived, they were twice the size of Lexi's mouth. I couldn't ram the huge ice-cold rings against Lexi's little gums, and she seemed distressed whenever I tried.

'Maybe we can't buy our way out of this,' Demi suggested as the pile of ineffective baby gadgets grew and grew. 'Maybe it's just about accepting things are different now. And that babies come with pain and difficulty.'

It's true. You can't really fix babies. No matter how much you spend on organic teething granules.

But if we couldn't buy our way out of this, how on earth would we cope?

#17 LIE – ONCE THEY START WEANING, THEY'LL SLEEP BETTER

Impatience and babies don't go very well together. This might sound obvious to you, a sensible person, but I've always been in a rush.

In my working life, I was an insane multitasker. I could write an email, brainstorm a plot, eat a cream-cheese bagel and phone my bank all at the same time, even sparing a little extra energy to ask the call representative why she needed my account number since I'd already inputted this on the numerical keypad before the call connected. Surely she had a record of this?

I got shit done. Quickly.

Babies, on the other hand, are sloooow. And you can't shout at babies to grow up faster – that's just bad parenting. Anyway, it doesn't work. No, I haven't tried it. Well, maybe once.

When Lexi hit five months, I wanted progress. Something to show we were getting somewhere and that all these nappy changes and menial labour weren't for nothing. Lexi was already sleeping through the night, but I had to tank her up on a lot of breast milk during the day, plus give her a 'dream feed' at 11 p.m. Now I wanted a proper night's sleep, all night, every night.

The baby-group midwives told me that when babies start weaning on to solid food, they can sleep from 7 p.m. to 7 a.m. all night, every night.

Weaning!

This sounded just the ticket.

They also advised not to wean until six months. But I gravitated towards internet sources that suggested it was OK to start a bit earlier as long as you went slowly.

It was a whole big political debate, it turned out. Is five months OK to wean? What about five and a half months? What if your baby is only four months old but weighed a stone at birth and is clearly starving hungry and making grabs for the KFC bargain bucket?

By and large, five months seemed OK to wean.

Idiotically, I decided to sidestep things like packets of baby rice, believing that healthy avocado was nature's glorious nutritional power-house and would be the ideal first weaning food.

I bought a high chair. Our already small dining area shrank by a third. Demi kindly returned the high chair and bought a little travel 'feeding' seat that sat on an existing dining chair and packed up for the car.

Lovely.

'Ooh, Lexi, a lovely new chair. Look, NEW chair. Chair!'

With Lexi strapped in place, I offered her spoonfuls of avocado. She ate and seemed to thoroughly enjoy it. I gave her some more.

Fantastic!

It all seemed so simple: food goes in; baby grows big and strong; baby sleeps longer at night.

Maybe that 'dream feed' would now be a thing of the past.

More calories equals longer sleep, right?

Wrong.

That night, Lexi woke at 9 p.m., midnight, 1 a.m., 3 a.m. and 5 a.m. I was extremely upset.

What the bejesus was going on?

Real proper food had been lovingly delivered. Why was she now waking up at all hours? Where was the logic here?

After obsessive internet scouring, I discovered the problem: avocado is hard for young babies to digest, hence the sensible suggestions of baby rice, pureed carrot, etc.

I bought a box of baby rice, fed Lexi the designated four spoonfuls and she slept better. But she still needed the dream feed and woke early. Nothing had really changed.

The next day, I mixed up the baby rice again, sat Lexi in her chair, fed her, washed everything down (including Lexi) and washed up. And the next day. And the next.

This was becoming a right pain in the arse and Lexi wasn't sleeping any differently to before. Also, I had to bring weaning food with us if we went out at lunchtime.

(Demi: 'Personally, I loved it when Lexi started weaning. Finally I could do something.')

Why on earth had I rushed? Why? I'd just set myself up for a lot more work a month sooner than I needed to.

Bollocks.

Lexi aged one, eating solid food from McDonald's. I'm a good mother. A good mother . . .

So began a hideous, messy time of horrible-looking vegetable purees stored in ice-cube trays, wallpaper-paste baby rice and glue-like baby porridge.

Pureed food all over clothes – mine, Demi's and Lexi's. Pureed food all over hair – mine, Demi's and Lexi's. Pureed food all over the buggy, lodged into crevices that could never be cleaned.

I realised how easy I'd had it with 'just breastfeeding' and hugely wished I could turn back time.

This was life with babies, I realised. Appreciate how shit you have it now, because it could get even shitter.

#18 LIE – IT'S BETTER WHEN THEY'RE BABIES – THEY DON'T TALK BACK!

By the time Lexi was six months, my state maternity pay had long since stopped, my savings had been spent on useless baby gadgets and I needed to get back to work.

This posed a problem. Who would look after Lexi while Demi and I were working?

We needed to find childcare.

All the good nurseries in Brighton (the ones with any kind of real greenery) were booked up years in advance.

Yes, *years*.

You had to get on the waiting list *before* you got pregnant.

Some nurseries still had spaces, but many weren't great. There was one around the corner from us. 'Safe House' it was called. Their USP was the prison-like security they kept children in all day long, combined with state-of-the-art CCTV monitoring. It had a concrete yard with barbed wire around its high walls and over fifty swivelling cameras that could be accessed via a secure weblink.

Every nursery, good or bad, had the same arrangement for babies: lines of barred beds in dark rooms for the under-ones, patrolled by young girls just out of vocational college. There was something of the Romanian orphanage about this set-up.

'What are we going to do?' I asked my sister. 'We're running out of money. I need to work, but Lexi seems too young for a nursery.'

'Are you sure she's too young?' said my sister. 'In Regency France, the aristocracy sent their babies to live in the countryside until they were three years old. The children only returned to their parents when they could speak enough French to tell the cook what they wanted for supper.'

'She just seems too young to be away from us,' I said. 'She's only a baby. She's too young to understand what's happening. She'll think we've abandoned her.'

'Peasants in Regency France worked with their babies beside them,' said my sister. 'Why don't you try working while Lexi sleeps?'

(It turns out my sister was researching Regency France at this time. She writes bestselling historical fiction as C. S. Quinn and is awesome. Read her books – they're fabulous.)

I thought about my sister's advice. Yes – work while Lexi slept. That seemed to be the only solution. Either that or financial difficulty.

Lexi's wet wipes, nappies, etc. didn't cost all that much, but with rent, bills, foolish baby-phase purchases, plus my sugar and hot-chocolate habit, our bank account was dropping to scarily low levels.

Why hadn't my parents been more sexist? Brought me up to be a docile female in pretty dresses and demand my husband take total financial responsibility for the household? Why had Demi and I been so right-on and created a life sharing rent and bills? Our liberal attitudes were coming back to haunt us.

As a freelance writer, I had no sick pay, holiday pay or full-pay maternity leave. I'd always earned enough to get by and no more. I hadn't really considered the future, believing myself to be too young to think about pensions and all that boring stuff.

When I thought about money, I got a crippling, anxious, sick feeling in my gut because I knew things were only just OK.

Our rent kept going up. Bills kept going up.

So I decided to follow my sister's advice and write while Lexi slept. Burn the candle at both ends and be one of those romantic rags-to-riches author success stories like J. K. Rowling.

While Lexi was napping, I dusted off my laptop and started looking through my inbox for freelance writing projects.

Unfortunately, something had happened to my brain. It had melted.

While I was struggling to read basic English, Lexi woke up.

There is nothing more distracting than a baby crying.

'She always sleeps for two hours after lunch,' I thought. 'Why would she wake up today of all days? When Mummy is trying to do business stuff.'

I phoned my sister and begged her to take Lexi out in the buggy so I could get on with the stressful business of conjuring money out of thin air.

My sister pointed out that in Regency France babies were simply swaddled and left until feeding time. But eventually, after a bit of a cry (me, not her), she agreed.

Cath took Lexi out and I sifted through my emails.

In the big pile was something from my agent. I'd submitted a novel to him a few months ago, but never expected anything to come of it because I'd been submitting that same novel in different forms for years.

I read the email.

Apparently, a publisher wanted my manuscript. Actually, not just that one manuscript. They wanted two manuscripts. I'd only gone and done it. I'd got the writer's holy grail: a publishing deal.

I should have been delighted. A publisher! At last! It was every writer's dream come true.

However, this was rather bad timing. All I could think was, 'How the fuck am I going to write a whole new book and look after a baby?'

'Maybe you should tell them you can't write a second book right now,' Demi reasoned. 'And do it next year.'

'Don't be fucking ridiculous!' I shouted. 'I've been waiting years to find a publisher. I WILL do that second book. I will find a way.'

I boiled up some strong coffee and tried to get going.

My sister returned with Lexi, who was wide awake and in playful spirits.

'She wouldn't sleep,' Cath explained. 'I thought she might be missing you.'

That's the thing about babies. They're so bloody unpredictable.

That evening, I phoned my mum and asked how she'd coped, working and looking after baby twins.

'Oh, I wouldn't call it coping,' Mum said. 'I just got on with it, and if I didn't cry at the end of the day, I counted myself lucky. But we had a childminder too. Remember Aunty Brenda?'

I did remember Aunty Brenda. She wasn't a real aunty, but a kindly red-headed childminder who looked after Cath and me as kids. She made us white-bread sandwiches, played eighties pop songs on the radio (from memory, that song was always 'Wake Me Up Before You Go-Go' by Wham) and taught us how to tie shoelaces. She was ever so nice.

Of course. A *childminder*.

Yes, that was the answer. Some nice lady who did childcare at home. So much gentler than leaving Lexi in a nursery room full of other babies.

We began our search for Mary Poppins.

Where I grew up in sunny, simple Essex, there was an abundance of smiley-faced grandmother types who liked nothing better than playing with, and mildly spoiling, children for a few pounds an hour.

Crazy, creative Brighton lacked these natural nurturers. It attracted bohemian, free-living artists, many of whom had addiction issues. Add to that the fact that city housing is extremely expensive and you get a disillusioned (possibly ex-drug addict) artist in a top-floor apartment, counting the hours until the toddlers running around her wrought-iron sculptures will go home to their real parents.

I interviewed a LOT of childminders. One freely admitted she didn't like children all that much. Another had an Ofsted complaint for giving a toddler cassoulet with wine in it.

Eventually we found a childminder who seemed cheerier than the rest. She had a small house, but everyone in Brighton has a small house. She was very nice and genuinely seemed to like children. Also, she had never killed or injured a child, according to her glowing Ofsted report.

We decided to go for it. Well, not decided. We had to go for it. Our choices were limited.

They say nothing can prepare you for having a baby. Well, additionally nothing prepares you for handing that baby over to someone else.

It felt far, far too soon. Years too soon. If only Lexi was older and could understand us and tell us how she was feeling, this would be so much easier.

I remember that fateful walk to the childminder's house for our first settling-in session.

Evil Brighton seagulls glided and swooped above us as I pushed Lexi's buggy down narrow streets, no doubt knowing she would soon be abandoned to their beaks and claws. Would the childminder protect Lexi from seagulls, as I would? What if the childminder left Lexi outside for a moment and one of the bigger birds – Beefy Bob as I called him – flew off with her? Just because there were no recorded cases of seagulls stealing children, didn't mean it couldn't happen.

I had tears in my eyes as I told Lexi that a lovely lady would look after her while Mummy worked.

Lexi didn't understand a word, of course. She just made 'bah bah bah' noises and chewed at the Gay Pride rainbow flag she'd recently made her treasured comforter.

We drew nearer to the childminder's house.

I considered doing a runner. I could take Lexi home and just forget about all this childminding business. Did we really need pricey accommodation with four walls and electricity? Couldn't we live off-grid somewhere in one of those tiny houses I'd been hearing so much about?

No. There was no way I was emptying my own composting toilet while caring for a young baby.

Reluctantly, I continued our journey.

Bad omens were everywhere during that ten-minute walk to the childminder's house. A single magpie flew overhead. A black cat skittered out of an alleyway. A drunk, homeless man staggered up the street going '*MAAAAH*'.

Eventually, we reached the childminder's house.

I knocked, half-expecting the witch from *Hansel and Gretel* to open the door and say, 'Have you been feeding the baby well, my dear? I like them nice and plump.'

But, of course, the pretty Italian childminder answered, all smiles and continental double-cheek kisses.

'Come in, come in,' she said. 'Let's get little Lexi settled.'

I proceeded to explain at length (again) how the settling-in session should go.

'And she always sleeps with this Gay Pride flag. And here are her food purees. She looks like she's spitting them out sometimes, but you just have to shove them back in . . .'

The childminder smiled calmly. 'Don't worry,' she said. 'I've done this before. She'll be very well taken care of.'

Yes, I thought. Obviously, she'll be well taken care of. That's a basic given. But will you do everything exactly as I do it?

Lexi started crying then.

'Don't worry.' The childminder took Lexi from me and gently swayed her. 'She'll be OK when you've gone.'

Lexi reached out her little arms for me and cried harder.

Ouch.

It was like having my heart ripped out.

Lexi had been by my side or in my arms for the last six months. She was almost part of my body. It felt too soon. She was so little. She wasn't ready. She couldn't understand what was happening.

Worse – I knew Lexi's surrogate carer wouldn't follow my 'advice' (instructions) to the letter.

Sensing my unease, the childminder said, 'The settling-in will only be a few hours today. Nothing bad can happen in just a few hours. What if you had surgery? You'd leave her with someone else then, wouldn't you?'

Yes, I thought. But I'd leave her with her dad, who knows her well. Obviously. What nonsense logic is that?

However, I knew the childminder was right. A few hours wouldn't hurt.

With an awful pain in my heart, I walked out of the door and tried to blot out Lexi's screams.

Lexi really went for it – I could hear her halfway up the street. As Judge Judy says, children are manipulative little beasts.

When I got to my computer, I was far too upset to work.

The only thing I wanted to do was run back to my little girl and snatch her back into my arms.

I hadn't thought about allowing extra work time for emotional turmoil.

I phoned Demi and cried some more.

He said in a whispery, worried voice, 'How badly was she crying? Did she sound *very* distressed?'

I confirmed Lexi had been *deeply* distressed.

We both decided we'd pick Lexi up a bit early. Just in case.

An hour later, we approached the childminder's house, ready for the big reunion.

'Lexi will be so happy to see us!' we decided.

I had images of Lexi crying the whole morning, calling out for us in her baby way, not understanding where her dear parents had gone. The poor lamb.

When we arrived at the childminder's door, we couldn't hear any crying.

'That's a good sign,' I told Demi. 'She was wailing her head off when I left.'

We knocked and waited.

There was no reply.

We knocked harder.

Still no reply.

Then we started to panic.

'Oh my god,' I said. 'What if something's happened?'

My already overly active imagination began doing its usual number on me, painting all the awful scenarios that could have happened to our young baby.

'I'll phone the childminder!' I screamed. 'Why would she be out? This is Lexi's nap time. She knows this is nap time – Lexi should be sleeping in the cot upstairs. The childminder wouldn't have left her alone, would she?'

We phoned, but there was no reply.

I have literally never felt panic like it. It was so severe I was immobilised by it. I couldn't move or think. I wanted to sit on the pavement and cry.

Then the childminder came trotting down the street with Lexi sleeping in the buggy.

'You're here early,' she remarked cheerfully, as she unlocked the front door. 'We've just been to the park. We had a little bit of a picnic and then Lexi fell asleep.'

I resisted the urge to ask exactly *when* Lexi had fallen asleep, how long she'd been asleep, what time she'd fed and what she'd eaten in grams and ounces.

Demi and I didn't admit we'd been idiotically panicking. We just thanked the childminder and told her we'd be back for another settling-in session tomorrow.

'It went very well,' said the childminder. 'She's a very contented baby.'

We smiled in that fake way you do when you know someone's bullshitting you for kind reasons.

We knew Lexi was not a contented baby, because she had two stressed, overanxious parents. But we were too polite to say so.

#19 LIE – BREASTFEEDING HELPS YOU LOSE WEIGHT

As I got back to work and joined the world of adult humans again, I decided to cut back on breastfeeding and replace Lexi's afternoon feed with formula.

I'd done my six months of only breast milk. More than six months, actually. Lexi was weaning now. It seemed like a good time to move towards boob freedom – especially now her teeth had come through (ouch).

Did I feel guilty about introducing one formula feed a day?

Yes.

Do I think that's ridiculous?

Yes.

But you know how us mothers are. We feel guilty about everything. I feel guilty right now being away from my kids and they're at *school*, for goodness' sakes. I'd actually be breaking the law if I spent time with them.

With breastfeeding on its way out, I had an uncomfortable reality to face up to.

I was now obese. Fat. I'd eaten all the pies. Become a chubby checker.

Breastfeeding had not been the magical weight-loss plan I had been sold.

The horrible, unforgiving scales told me I was 37 per cent fat.

If you're not familiar with fat percentages, I'll sum that up for you: fucking fat.

(Demi: 'I was also fat at this time. No, I'm not saying you were fat. No, no, no. No, you weren't fat. I was fat. Very fat. That's what I meant.')

That thing about breastfeeding helping you 'naturally' lose weight without really trying? It doesn't work if you're a hot-chocolate and biscuit addict.

I'd got through the pregnancy (morning sickness, piles, weird stuffy nose), the first horrible bit of breastfeeding (cracked nipples, mastitis, general pain) and THIS was my reward: a body that looked like I was wearing a comedy fat suit.

Here were my stats by the time I stopped breastfeeding:

- 5' 7"
- 12 stone 6.6 lbs
- 37 per cent body fat
- A big, wobbly, squidgy stomach with loads of loose skin, and that horrible pregnancy brown line down the middle
- 37¾ inches around the middle
- Chafing body parts
- A double chin

I kept waiting for my pregnant-looking stomach to deflate like a giant balloon, but it never happened.

My mum kept taking sideways glances at me, asking if I was carrying extra packets of wet wipes in my sweatshirt pockets.

Eventually, reality was inescapable.

My stomach was not going to deflate any more.

It was not made of post-baby air.

It was fat.

When I finally stepped on the scales, post-baby, it really was a shock. I'd expected to put on a *bit* of weight. You know, *baby* weight. A few extra pounds that breastfeeding would certainly get rid of in time. But nearly thirty pounds over my normal weight? Wow. This was a whole extra person.

After a tiny bit of a cry, I decided this could actually be good news. Maybe if I lost weight, I could get my old body back. My saggy middle really might snap back into shape, giving me a toned, tanned abdomen.

It could happen.

I watched *The Real Housewives of Orange County*. Those women looked buff and some of them had *three* kids.

Diets sound simple when you're reading about them. But a few hours in, when you realise your chocolate-biscuit consumption is now heavily restricted, they become a good deal trickier.

Still, I was determined to lose some weight. I was sure I'd feel more like my old self if I shed a few pounds, but I knew dieting would be hard with a young baby. Sugar and tiredness go together like, well, Ben and Jerry. Häagen and Dazs. So I decided to join a fat club for middle-aged women.

You know the sort of club I mean – there are dozens of them. You *can* eat delicious food. Here are some pictures of delicious food. We'll show you how you can eat all this delicious food and lose weight! Now come and get humiliatingly weighed once a week and chit-chat with other fat women.

My first fat-club meeting was exactly as I had imagined. It was held in a dusty church hall (of course), and every lady who walked through the door was weighed on public scales.

There was a table of artificially sweetened snacks for sale, including chocolate-brownie bars, biscuits and juice – none of which could possibly foster good dietary habits. Still, the fat-club members were buying them in bulk, forming a long queue to get hold of these aspartame-laden goodies. Better stock up, I thought, before those chocolate-brownie bars run out.

The group leader was a jolly lady who'd lost a lot of weight and therefore had the requisite skills to lead us on our fat-to-thin journey. To be fair, she was still a bit chubby. But from what I gather, she had been hugely fat before and had needed specially fitting boots.

Along with useful weight-loss tips, our fat-club leader taught us fun, low-calorie drinking games and gave us warnings whenever a chocolate product had changed its sizing.

During the first meeting, I was given my calorie ration for the day. And a small fat-club biscuit to take home.

Breastfeeding allowed me an extra chocolate bar a day, but this didn't help much because I was used to eating three extra chocolate bars a day, plus drinking a LOT of hot chocolate.

I needed to take control of myself. Exercise some restraint. Just as soon as I'd eaten my rationed piece of chocolate and all those chocolate-brownie bars.

I left the meeting with a healthy-eating book, some new fellow-obese friends and a determination to shift thirty pounds and find my inner Beyoncé – tanned and toned after having kids.

Once home, I threw out all the crap food: frozen pizza, garlic bread, cans of tomato soup, bags of jelly fried-egg and foamy raspberry sweets and, most heartbreakingly, a metre-long novelty chocolate bar I'd been working my way through.

I then filled the cupboards with low-fat, artificially sweetened, fat-club products.

Demi was appalled. He would have eaten all that stuff I'd thrown out, he said. Why waste food like that? Why not give it to people? Where were my eco-credentials? And what was with all the fake, sweetened crap?

'You don't understand,' I whined. 'I don't have self-control like you do. If high-calorie food is in the house, I'll eat it. Even from the bin.'

Demi offered to hide unhealthy items, but I knew this wouldn't work since I'd long been familiar with all his hiding places.

After a quick row, I downloaded the fat-club app so I could calculate every calorie from now on. I bought lots of vegetables and tried to exercise more, squeezing in hot-yoga classes when Lexi had gone to bed.

Pleasingly, the weight started to shift.

I upped my vegetables and even more weight began to shift. When I ran out of fake, high-carb, sweetened fat-club products, the weight practically fell off.

It took a few months and some humiliating public weigh-ins, calorie-restricted tiredness, rage and depression, but I finally shed twenty pounds. And I really did feel better. Much better. Less tired and cow-like. I was still two sizes bigger than pre-Lexi, but I could run upstairs without huffing and puffing.

However, there was some bad news. My stomach hadn't sprung back to shape like an elastic band. My thighs had not become magically smooth and tanned. I did not look like Beyoncé.

I had lost weight, but I had to accept that my body had changed forever. My stomach would never be flat again. My boobs – let's not even go there. Just whisper: older.

Yes, my youthful body had gone. Just gone.

Clothes-wise, I was in a weird no man's land. My pre-pregnancy clothes didn't fit, but Topshop and H&M didn't sell anything that flattered my new, older body. So I just carried on wearing maternity stuff and Demi's sweatshirts.

I should have gone out and bought a new wardrobe of clothes right then and there. I should have transformed, grown up. Embraced my new life and body. But I couldn't accept maturity just yet.

I mean, honestly, who wants to embrace big old-lady pants in their early thirties?

Growing up looked rubbish.

#20 LIE – YOU'LL ENJOY IT MORE AFTER THE FIRST YEAR

As Lexi reached her first year, the pressure really began to build.

Demi and I were both working, juggling baby care and the occasional interrupted night's sleep, while living somewhere unsuitable for a family.

Our apartment was noisy, slightly damp, dark and cramped. Plus, our proximity to the chaotic, hard-partying city centre came at a premium. We were paying thousands of pounds a month to live somewhere with sick on the pavements.

People were always chucking beer cans in our front garden, and one evening a couple had sex in our porch.

We still hadn't got the memo: 'This isn't a family-friendly location.'

With me working part-time (although life is never *part-time* when you have kids) while getting the second novel finished, and Demi working full-time as a freelance songwriter, we had enough money to get by. Sometimes.

(Demi: 'I also had a part-time job as a phone monkey and was finishing a sports journalism course. Just saying. I was doing a lot. Yes, I know you were too.')

It all depended on Demi's commissions. If he got a big songwriting project – great. But at slow times of year things were tough. We dreaded summer and Christmas, when everyone goes on holiday and stops commissioning.

The trick was not to think too much about the future (and possible rent increases) as that brought about major anxiety.

Life became survival. I'd get through the night praying not to be woken too often. Then I'd ferry Lexi to the childminder, bid an emotional farewell, work through my lunch break, pick Lexi up and try to fit in a few more hours' work during her afternoon nap.

We were existing, but not in a joyful way. The combination of freelance employment, the expensive and crowded city living and our small, unsuitable apartment was taking its toll.

Demi and I should have moved to a nice family home before the birth, of course. We should have had responsible jobs with maternity leave and sick pay. We should have understood why parents have gardens with trampolines in them. But we threw ourselves into parenthood prepared for babies but not family life, and now we were too tired to make major changes.

Life was stressful.

Things weren't quite as dark and awful as the early days, but life felt overwhelming and unrewarding. There was no finish line, no prize for having a baby scream in your face for hours. No financial bonus for working all day on five hours' sleep. Just less money and more exhaustion.

We hadn't yet reached our happy ending.

To top it all off, sometimes Lexi cried for two hours at a time without stopping, and if that doesn't raise your blood pressure then you're technically dead.

Because Demi and I hadn't yet embraced parenthood in a meaningful way, we coped with stress the same way we did pre-children.

We drank alcohol.

Now Lexi was eating solid food and I was breastfeeding less, I could cheerfully imbibe seven units of alcohol at night without poisoning my baby. This was based on a mathematical calculation that considered units of alcohol, weight, height, gender and ethnicity.

Just to make really sure I'd got the calculation right, I bought some special paper that tested alcohol in breast milk. The paper turned a tarry black colour if evil alcohol was present in breast milk, but it only ever turned a light grey for me – even if I tested directly after drinking a glass of wine. It was always snowy white a few hours after drinking.

My first conclusion: not much alcohol goes into breast milk. (But don't take my word for it. I'm not a doctor.)

My second conclusion: you can drink a whole bottle of wine, go to sleep, and your boobs will be booze-free in the morning.

I'm not saying I *did* drink a whole bottle of wine every night. But it was nice to know I could.

Of course, there would be no more banging shots of tequila any more, now we had the responsibility for a little life. No. Wine was the thing. Sophisticated wine. I even bought wine glasses.

Some evenings, Lexi had a fever or molar teething pain and took two hours to scream herself to sleep. This sent our stress levels sky-high.

'We should get some wine,' one of us would say, an eyelid twitching. 'I'm heading down to the supermarket.'

'Make sure it's thirteen per cent or higher,' the other would shout with a little pretend laugh to cover up the seriousness of this request.

Before kids, alcohol had been a casual 'let's all go out and have fun!' kind of thing. Now it was medicine for stress. A much-needed relaxant. A necessity rather than an enjoyment.

Take away all the stylish glassware and you were essentially left with a painkiller. Something to lower our ever-growing stress levels.

Often, I'd reassure myself that we weren't drinking for the wrong reasons. We were sophisticated parents, just having a few glasses of wine in the evening, as many moderate people do.

We'd lay out cheese and wasabi nuts on our Freecycle coffee table, just to make everything feel more like a gastropub experience rather than an ugly drug addiction.

Then we'd down our first glass of wine within ten minutes.

'The first drink always goes down quickly,' we'd chuckle. 'We're very stressed.'

Half an hour later, our second glass would be empty again.

'You don't get many glasses in a bottle, do you?' we'd observe.

One of us would tentatively offer to 'pop out and get another bottle'.

'YES!' the other would shout.

The 'bottle of wine each on a Friday and Saturday' ritual soon became a weekend tradition. And sometimes it wandered into week-days too.

I found myself wondering what counted as 'too early' to start drinking.

Seven p.m. was clearly fine – this was middle-class dinnertime, and everyone knows people have a glass of wine with their meal.

Six o'clock? Getting a bit less respectable, but there is such a thing as an aperitif, is there not? I'd been to Italy. Italians have big glasses of Aperol before their leisurely evening meals.

Five o'clock was clearly too early. Or was it?

Summer was approaching, and Brighton was having all sorts of open-air family festivals. These tended to include Prosecco tents, locally produced cider stalls and other 'grown-up' ways to drink alcohol. You often saw parents sitting on geometric-patterned blankets, drinking from fun glassware.

If other people were doing it, surely it was OK.

Were we technically sitting on a bench, drinking cider at midday?

Yes, *technically*. But this was organic, locally brewed cider with an authentic apple smell and taste.

We were parents, for goodness' sake! Of course this was entirely respectable. And a medical necessity for stress.

At one year of age, Lexi had passed through the rolling-over, sitting-up, teething, weaning and crawling phases. She was now entering the 'baby walk around and wreck things' phase.

Every passing day, things like a broken mug or a ripped-up book reinforced how small and unsuitable our home really was.

The storage heaters couldn't be turned off, so were burning hot and ready for Lexi to stumble upon. Unless, of course, we needed some actual warmth in the house. Then they would inexplicably be stone cold. The kitchen was only big enough for one person, which made Lexi a trip hazard.

Demi and I were dimly aware that our house wasn't suitable for a one-year-old vandal. But was it really bad enough to move? We had friends living in far worse places. Our neighbour lived in a similar flat to ours and had four kids. Yes, *four*.

Moving house seemed drastic. And extremely tiring.

Before Lexi came along, Demi and I had been delighted with our apartment. What could be more perfect? Friends upstairs. The rent wasn't too bad for Brighton. It was a little dark and dingy, sure, but it was somewhere to hang our hats and our Arsenal scarfs.

Every piece of furniture we owned was second-hand (one accidentally stolen, as mentioned), and the most decorative we got was sticking a load of coloured pencils together to make an interesting wall feature.

But as Lexi got bigger and we got larger gadgets (the Bumbo seat, the VTech baby walker, the Scuttlebug, the big baby bed), our feelings about 'home sweet home' changed.

It was clear we were stuffing family life into a young couple's pad. And not a sophisticated couple's pad either. A crap one.

The apartment had been right for carefree twenty-somethings who weren't bothered about thin, cheap carpets and mouldy showers. But when you have a baby, you want cleanliness. A toilet that flushes properly. And space – lots and lots of space.

Our unsuitable home seemed even more unsuitable when we visited the homes of our new maternity-group friends. These sensible souls had climbed the property ladder in their early twenties while we had been out getting drunk. They had planned not just for pregnancy and newborns, but for a life beyond. Family life.

Our 'new parent' friends had lovely, cosy, child-friendly homes with modern cooking facilities, nursery rooms and neat little gardens with spongy alphabet tiles covering hard concrete areas. They had new furniture, Dyson vacuum cleaners and furniture polish in plastic caddies under the sink.

These grown-up family spaces were a stark contrast to our orange-and-brown flat, with its retro cooker, brown wallpaper and semi-ironic 'shit hole' poster in the lounge.

Not only had our antenatal friends *already bought and decorated* family homes, but they had jobs with maternity leave and pension plans. This was proper adult stuff.

In contrast, we had stumbled into pregnancy as feckless freelancers.

I had no maternity leave, believing I could 'work around' the baby. Our home was a one-bedroom rental property. We didn't have a car or a tumble dryer or Ikea click-together storage.

The more time we spent at home (and we were home a LOT now), the more everything felt wrong.

The storage heaters, which had previously amused us with their bizarre heat conduction, were now irritating enough to be kicked and shouted at regularly.

The damp, windowless hallway was oppressive.

The concrete and rock yard, formerly admired for its cheeky resident fox, was now full of dangerous steps and jagged edges. And who's to say foxes don't eat babies? Who really knew for sure?

Plus, our apartment was noisy at night, thanks to our child-free friends upstairs, enjoying the life we used to have.

The selfish bastards.

I was usually good at forward planning. How had I made this massive oversight? How had we careered into this new life without any of the necessary infrastructure?

In hindsight, we were both naive and delusional. Neither Demi nor I realised just how much of ourselves would have to change to have a family. People had warned us, but we had ignored them.

We were free-thinking, creative types, unencumbered by houses and cars and all that jazz, man. We thought outside the box. Why conform to a cookie-cutter family life when we didn't conform to anything else? We're not dead yet!

We wanted kids, but we also wanted our fun, quirky, independent lives in the city.

We didn't realise we couldn't have both.

We were stupid.

It was becoming very clear now: having a baby was not a 'slot into your life' sort of deal. Kids don't slot into your life. They smash your life to pieces and you have to rebuild it on their terms.

Everything had to change.

If parenthood has taught me anything, it's this: if you don't embrace change – if you refuse to grow, if you try and cling to the past – life will become painful. And soon the pain will be so bad that you'll be forced to change because you can't stand it any more.

(You might want to highlight that profound statement.)

One afternoon, after Lexi had torn up my new copy of *Heat* magazine, I had an epiphany/meltdown.

It was the day of the royal wedding, when Prince William and Kate Middleton married in a dazzling, romantic *(Demi: 'and expensive burden on the taxpayer')* ceremony.

I had taken Lexi to see the royal wedding at our local Wetherspoons pub because Demi, a strident republican, refused to have it on our TV.

When Lexi and I arrived home, someone had thrown a beer can and an empty packet of cheese Doritos (jumbo size) in the front garden.

People were always doing that.

I did the usual front-garden litter-pick as Lexi fidgeted and cried in the buggy. Then I went through the faff of folding the buggy, putting the rain cover over it and bike-locking it to the gas pipe outside, all while trying not to drop my young daughter.

When we got inside, I found Demi moving fans around, trying to get some cool air flowing through the windowless hall.

The bedroom looked impossibly full with the bed, cot, changing table and various baby toys.

'The cooker isn't working again,' said Demi. 'I've phoned the letting agents, but they won't fit a new one. Not until all four rings stop working.'

I started to cry.

'We don't fit here any more,' I said.

'I've been thinking that too,' said Demi. 'The trouble is, I don't know where we do fit.'

We had a cup of tea and a think about things.

'What about moving nearer my family?' I suggested, remembering Mum's sensible words about family homes in Essex (and strategically forgetting that I'd sworn at her). 'To my home town, where houses are less expensive.'

Demi did not like this suggestion. 'I'm not living in Essex,' he said. 'It's racist and full of Greggs bakeries.'

'Essex isn't *that* racist,' I insisted. 'And Greggs bakeries do filter coffee now.'

'How would you know it's not that racist?' said Demi. 'You're white. No one is going to be racist to you.'

'They were. In Costa Rica – they thought I was American.'

'Not the same.'

'It is!'

We had another cup of tea and a bit more of a think.

'Maybe we don't really need to move,' I decided. 'We're going through a stressful time, but things get easier after the first year. Everyone always says that about kids.'

It's true. Everyone is always saying that about kids. But it didn't feel like things were getting easier. If anything, the stresses were mounting up.

'The city is OK for kids really,' said Demi. 'If you ignore all the cars and noise and queues.'

We thought about Brighton's quirky shops, the cinema that sold gourmet hot dogs, the pairs of shoes artfully thrown over electricity lines. But all these things were uninteresting to young children and were also surrounded by busy roads and swarms of drunk twenty-somethings.

'It just doesn't feel right any more,' I said.

'So what is right?' Demi asked.

Neither of us knew.

#21 LIE – BABY-LED WEANING IS MUCH EASIER

So we were stuck. Trapped in a life that didn't suit us any more, but not knowing how to move forwards. We didn't want to leave the city. We *loved* the city. But it wasn't right for us now.

What should we do?

We didn't know.

And then something happened that made up our minds for us.

A chickpea.

Before you laugh, this is a serious business. Life-threatening, even.

One day (my birthday, to be precise – but who cares about your birthday when you have kids?), I was wandering around one of Brighton's many organic supermarkets, prodding the spelt loaves and wondering why people buy goat's milk yoghurt (something to do with lactose digestion, apparently).

It was nearly lunchtime and Lexi was getting grizzly. She was just over one, fully weaned on to solid food and these days she needed a full meal at lunchtime – preferably something hot.

I thought about the leaky Tupperware tub rattling around under the buggy. It contained last night's lasagne, mashed into a revolting meaty paste.

I'll have to get that out and give Lexi lunch in a minute, I thought. *What a pain in the arse. I wish we could go back to just breastfeeding.*

Then I remembered about baby-led weaning. I'm sure you know what this is, but if you don't, let me describe it for you: 'Purees and mashed foods are unnecessary. You don't need to blend anything. Babies can suck and gnaw at whole food items, like bread and fruit. Their little gums will mash everything up and eventually the food will disintegrate. Much less work for you, only make sure you cover your child, the high chair, floor and yourself with five metres of wipe-clean plastic.'

I could try that baby-led weaning today, I thought. *It sounds a lot easier than messing around with lasagne mush.*

At this point we were swinging by the fresh-beans aisle (they have those in organic supermarkets) and a shop attendant offered us a raw soaked chickpea.

'Perfect!' I said. 'A little snack to keep us going. Lexi, suck on this while I prod the spelt bread.'

I gave Lexi the chickpea, imagining it to be soft and yielding.

I was wrong.

It turns out soaked chickpeas are as hard as nuts.

Lexi began to choke, wheeze and turn bright red.

It's true what they say about awful things happening in slow motion. I remember every second of Lexi choking, and the overwhelming panic and powerlessness.

Lexi turned redder and redder, her throat rasping, her eyes wide with terror.

It was awful. The absolute worst moment of my life.

'Help!' I begged the wide-eyed deli man. 'Call an ambulance!'

The deli-counter man threw down his large olive spoon, pulled a mobile phone from his striped apron and placed the emergency call in three seconds flat.

Moments later an ambulance sped to a halt outside the supermarket.

Thank you, deli-counter man. Thank you, NHS.

The paramedic team put an oxygen mask on Lexi and shone a torch in her mouth.

'She's getting a significantly reduced amount of oxygen,' they said. 'But she's still breathing. She'll have to come into hospital immediately. What has she got stuck down there?'

'A chickpea,' I said.

'A what?'

'A chickpea. It's a type of bean. They use them in hummus.'

The paramedics discussed this and confirmed the hospital would have something for organic-bean removal. After all, this was Brighton.

Lexi and I were rushed to A&E, but as soon as the staff realised Lexi wasn't dying, just rasping like an angry cat, we were quickly dispatched to the non-emergency part of the hospital and settled in for a long wait.

After eight hours, a paediatric doctor checked Lexi over.

By then it was 7 p.m. and Lexi was falling asleep. She'd stopped rasping a while ago, so I assumed the chickpea must have moved around a bit.

The doctor took a good look in Lexi's throat but couldn't see anything. He decided Lexi must have coughed up or swallowed the chickpea. Or perhaps the chickpea had never been there in the first place.

'It definitely was in her throat,' I said. 'She was choking. Could it have gone into her lung?'

The doctor gave me a long, hard look that said, 'You're one of those anxious first-time mums who abuse overworked medical staff, aren't you?'

'Well, where else could it have gone?' I queried. 'If she was choking, it was stuck in her windpipe, right?'

'Unlikely to have gone into her lung,' said the doctor. 'If you *want* to stay in hospital, you'll just be wasting everyone's time.'

I was incensed by this.

Of course I didn't *want* to stay in hospital. It was my birthday and I had two cans of pina colada cocktail waiting in the fridge. Lexi *always* slept between 7 p.m. and 7 a.m., I told the doctor, thus allowing me to drink up to seven units of alcohol before the next breastfeed. My golden drinking hours were quietly slipping away with every moment that passed.

The doctor said, 'Well, you should probably get going, then. It's gone 7 p.m. already.'

> *(Demi: 'May I just point out, I was also at the hospital. Just in case anyone thinks I took a back seat. I also offered to go home and get Su's pina colada, since she kept going on about it. She said she felt socially awkward about drinking alcohol in hospital while holding her sick child.')*

The next day, Lexi's chest was bad.

We were very worried.

I took Lexi to the doctor, but he told me to stop being over anxious.

More days passed and Lexi's chest got worse and worse.

Soon Lexi started to cough all night long – a big, hacking smoker's cough.

The doctors kept saying it was a chest infection, but I knew better. It was that cursed chickpea. What else could it be?

After various X-rays and PET scans, one specialist eventually found mucus growth and 'matter' in Lexi's lung.

'It's a chickpea!' I said. 'A rotten, old chickpea!'

'Well, whatever it is, it needs to come out,' said the specialist. 'She's going to need an operation. In the meantime, you should stay out of damp environments to stop the infection getting worse and causing permanent lung damage.'

I thought about our flat with the green mould growing above the shower, and the black mould in the windowless hallway.

'Do green patches mean somewhere is damp?' I asked.

'Yes,' said the doctor. 'And a mouldy environment is certainly one you should stay away from.'

When we returned home, I called our letting agents to berate them about our dangerously damp apartment.

To their credit, they immediately sent round a comedy builder duo who knocked a hole in our wall to fit an extractor fan.

'Oh no, no, no, Kevin. You've gone and knocked half the blimmin' wall out. I can put my arm through that hole. See?'

'I thought we were taking the wall down.'

'NO, son. Not the whole wall. We're putting in an extractor fan.'

'What's a tractor fan?'

The extractor fan, when it was finally fitted, made absolutely no difference to the damp air. If anything, it seemed to let more damp air in.

'We need to move house,' I told Demi. 'We don't have a choice.'

'But where?' said Demi. 'We've been checking Rightmove for months. The only thing we can afford are basement apartments. They'll be damper than here.'

'We need a proper family house with nice, dry, upstairs bedrooms,' I said. 'It's time to buy a place. Then rent will stop going up. We'll make it work somehow.'

I spent a few days looking into mortgages.

There was good news and bad. The good news was we could afford a property in Brighton's fashionable, affluent Kemp Town district. The bad news was that property would be a garage.

There seemed only one option left: leave the city and its dazzling array of fairy-light shops, bagel bakeries, milkshake parlours and bubble-tea emporiums.

But didn't we love all that stuff? Wouldn't we be ever so sad without the buzz and creativity of city life?

Demi and I considered this.

Every day with a one-year-old was a busy, crowded, expensive, unfriendly struggle. Life was a gruelling groundhog day, pushing Lexi along noisy, polluted streets to the childminder's house, working all day in a cramped freelancer office, then sitting in our dark, miserable apartment all evening long. And don't get me started on the post office queue – it took *hours* to send a parcel.

Maybe we didn't love city life any more.

We were at a crisis point. A jump-or-be-pushed moment. That thing that happens to heroes in all good movies. It was time to take a big, brave leap into the unknown. To start building the new life we should have built a while ago. The happily-ever-after.

Demi and I began scouring Rightmove for affordable family homes in small towns near Brighton.

Our budget didn't stretch very far. We could afford two bedrooms, but not two bedrooms that fitted whole beds in them.

'Why don't we search properties in my home-town area?' I suggested. 'Just to see what comes up?'

Demi muttered about 'racist Essex' but let me put the search into Rightmove.

We were in for a shock.

A good shock.

'These houses are in our price range?' said Demi. 'They have *driveways*.'

'And gardens!' I added excitedly. 'This one has a *shed*.'

'Are you absolutely sure you've put the search terms in correctly?' said Demi. 'You haven't accidentally added an extra nought on the budget?'

'Positive.'

'Are these houses in the middle of nowhere or something?' Demi asked.

'No,' I said. 'Right in the centre of the village.'

'A VILLAGE!' Demi had finally found the snag. 'So that's why they're so cheap.'

'It's a large village just outside my home town,' I said. 'Because you said you didn't want to be in a racist town.'

'A village sounds boring,' said Demi.

'Maybe that's what we need,' I said. 'Peace and quiet. We hardly ever go out. We're tired by 9 p.m. We watch BBC dramas. Perhaps it's time we accept reality. Look – these are light, bright family homes with upstairs bedrooms. No damp air!'

We'd been struggling for so long, paying sky-high rent for a damp little box in Brighton. It was hard to believe there was anything better for us. But it seemed there was if we were brave enough to take a flying leap into something new.

I booked some house viewings and at the end of the week Lexi and I met an aftershave-fumed estate agent on the driveway of a four-bedroom property in Wivenhoe (Americans – you may snigger here at silly British village names).

The sun was shining as we walked up the driveway, past spring flowers and a jaunty little wheelbarrow full of daffodils.

Fucking hell.

Compared to our Brighton place, this house was massive. You'd literally pay millions for this in the city.

Also, the surroundings were green and peaceful. No car noise. No screeching drunk people. I doubted anyone had sex in these porches and there were no empty beer cans either.

'This is the place?' I asked the estate agent. 'It's enormous.'

The estate agent raised a doubtful eyebrow. 'It's just a 1970s semi.'

'But it's got a *garage*.'

'They all do around here.'

'And a dining room.'

'Well, where else would you eat your meal?'

'On the sofa with a plate on your knees?'

The estate agent gave an amused chuckle. But of course, I wasn't joking.

'The owner is home for our visit,' said the estate agent. 'So please don't say anything negative about the house. The last couple laughed at the carpets.'

As if I would! I didn't care if the inside of this property was covered with used syringes – we were taking it. Of course, I didn't tell the estate agent this. That would have been poor bartering.

We went inside the house and I oohed and aahed at the cupboard under the stairs, the loft hatch, the bath, the airing cupboard and the garden shed.

Wow.

The house was styled at a time when *Dallas* was popular and it boasted heavily lacquered dark-wood kitchen cabinets, wedding-cake swirly Artex, wood-chip wallpaper and a gas fire surrounded by patio slabs.

Retro cool, right? Even better, the house didn't feel in the tiniest bit damp. All it needed was a lick of paint here, a wall knocked down there.

The elderly owner whispered, 'The couple before you talked about knocking down walls. And I thought to myself, *I'm not selling my house to you!*

I laughed politely and decided to keep quiet about any renovation plans, telling a white lie about the 'nice' salmon-pink carpets.

Decor aside, I was blown away by the property. There was so much space. This was luxury living, no matter what the estate agent had to say about it.

'We'll take it,' I said.

'Don't you want to ask your husband first?' asked the nice lady owner. 'Or come back for a second viewing?'

'Oh no,' I assured her. 'We don't have time for all that. And my husband usually goes along with whatever I want these days or I cry.'

(Demi: 'Yes, you have started doing that.')

'OK,' she said uncertainly.

When I got home, I told Demi the good news.

'Lexi and I found a house today,' I said. 'You like *Dallas*, don't you? And it's got stairs and an airing cupboard and a loft. I've told the owner we'll take it. That's OK, isn't it?'

Demi is an easy-going fellow.

'All right,' he said. 'Sure.'

Were we making a terrible decision and possibly ruining our lives? Neither of us knew. But we'd run out of choices a long time ago.

PART III: TO SUFFER IS TO GROW

#22 LIE – YOUR STRETCHMARKS WILL GO EVENTUALLY. USE COCOA BUTTER!

Soon we were packing boxes, redirecting mail and swearing at conveyancers for their slow, slow house-sale progress.

As I filled boxes with a lifetime of possessions, I noted the many items we'd bought before Lexi was born. The oversized St Patrick's Day squishy top hat. The beer pong game. The novelty pineapple sunglasses and the Jack Daniels shot glasses.

We hadn't used that stuff in a while. Should we bag it all up and throw it out?

No.

One day, some day – when Lexi was older – we would need these things again. Right? We would drunkenly sing again one St Patrick's Day, wearing that large bright-green top hat. We would attend a Hawaiian-themed party and wear those novelty pineapple sunglasses again one day. We would return to this city.

We would come back and reclaim our old life when Lexi was older and we had more money.

In the meantime, we would store these things in the new loft. We have a loft!

With every packed box, the past faded like a photo in the sun.

I thought about all the dear friends we'd be leaving behind. Our lovely maternity gang. Other friends we'd got elaborately drunk with, pre-children.

It was a sad business. A very sad business. Sure, we'd be moving nearer my parents, who were absolutely ecstatic about our return to sunny Essex. But most of my childhood friends had moved away.

'Don't worry,' Demi reassured me. 'You'll meet lots of new people. It's easy when you have kids.'

Shit, I thought. New people.

It was high time I stopped dressing like a sofa-lounging invalid and more like a responsible adult.

For the last year, I'd been slouching around in oversized sports clothes, my hair pulled into a badly combed shark-finned ponytail.

The parents in this quiet, rural location didn't know me pre-baby. They wouldn't know I'd once been a human being.

I really needed to sort myself out and start dressing like a functioning adult.

Think more responsible mother, less hobo troll.

During my pregnancy, I'd refused to buy the standard maternity clothes, instead buying size-eighteen dresses from Topshop, oversized eighties rock vests, and leggings from H&M.

Why were maternity clothes so *sensible*, I'd wondered. I'm pregnant, not *dead*. Where is the leopard print? The hot pink? Even the maternity jeans had dark-blue turn-ups and creases ironed down the front. Where were the rips? The studs?

Now, with a more mature, motherly figure and a young baby to look after, I understood. Despite slapping cocoa butter on my wrinkly stomach for the past year, I still had an abundance of loose skin. No amount of dieting or exercise would get rid of it, and the cocoa butter made absolutely no difference.

My body shape had changed. I now had sticky-out, saggy bits that did not look good in tight clothing.

When I opened my wardrobe, I saw clothing for a young girl who sat around on the beach, drinking beer. Who went to festivals and the pub. Who wore tight jeans. Whose stomach wasn't all saggy and stretched.

My old style was good for a twenty-something at a party with a reasonably slim figure.

I was no longer a twenty-something at a party. Or reasonably slim.

A remarkable ageing process had taken place. Something had happened to my body *and* face. The stress of a newborn had drained the youth out of me and I had suddenly plunged into middle age. My droopier, fatter body needed comfortable, forgiving clothes – absolutely no squeezed waistlines.

Lycra and neon were no longer my friends (if they ever had been). Oh no. They only highlighted my new, lumpier middle. Think *stretched*, *unflattering* and *mutton*.

I needed to get with the programme. Dress the body I had, not the one I wanted.

Subtle, mature, stylish, grown up – that was the thing. Clothes that made me look and feel well groomed. That didn't cling to my middle.

I needed a *Pretty Woman* moment.

Cue montage.

Flinging open my wardrobe, I made an honest assessment of my clothes.

I decided that most, if not all, of my pre-pregnancy clothing had to go. I'd been waiting for my body to 'ping' back into shape, but that clearly was not going to happen, no matter how much weight I lost.

Anything tight and polyester went straight in the charity bag, as did almost everything from H&M, Topshop, New Look and Forever 21.

Skinny jeans I didn't have a hope in hell of doing up – into the bag. Teeny-tiny lacy knickers that only served to highlight my now-roomier bottom, be gone. Bye-bye, novelty zig-zag, hot-pink and zebra-striped pull-up socks. Away with you.

I'd had fun wearing that stuff. But it wasn't who I was any more. And it made me look really unattractive.

If someone had told me that I'd throw this stuff out when I became a mother, I would have shouted at them: 'No, I won't! Why can't a mum have fun, youthful clothing? Why do we have to fit into a sensible mould? Why can't we be whoever we want, just because we have kids?'

I still think that.

I still believe people should be able to wear whatever they like. But in my case, those brightly coloured party clothes looked really bad on me.

I filled two huge bin bags for the charity shop, then assessed my now almost empty wardrobe. Hangers dangled in empty space, inviting a whole new life.

For a long time, I'd been hiding my body under leggings, Demi's big sweatshirts and an army jacket.

It was the look of someone trapped between two worlds. Someone refusing to accept that life had changed. Someone having an internal crisis, living in a world of turmoil.

I didn't want to look like that any more.

The trouble was I had no idea where to get new clothes. If Topshop and H&M were off limits, where else was there?

I would not – repeat, *not* – shop in Laura Ashley.

Good advice was needed.

I asked my maternity-mum friends, who all looked respectable yet still pretty cool, where they bought clothes.

They recommended Gap, Zara, Next, Boden and very occasionally Marks & Spencer.

I'd never bothered with these shops before, thinking of them as for older women.

Time for a rethink.

I hit town with Lexi strapped tightly into the buggy and bought myself some comfortable boyfriend-style jeans, Converse, asymmetric sweatshirts and pastel-coloured hoodies.

The standard modern-mother wardrobe. Boring, right? But actually it was flattering and made me feel good when I looked in the mirror.

I bought a few 'going out' items too, but nothing as flashy and synthetic as before. Nice, loose, stylish dresses made of grown-up fabrics like silk and wool.

When I got home, I put on a new 'daytime casual' outfit – flattering peddle-pusher jeans, a striped top and white Converse.

The clothes felt clean and comfortable, like just-laundered cotton.

When I looked in the mirror, I saw a well-dressed adult. A parent, but a young one.

I felt like a new person.

Excellent.

Next, I assessed my hair, which had been pulled back into an 'I can't be bothered to do my hair today' ponytail since Lexi came along. The home-dyed blonde streaks had long since grown out, leaving a boring mid-brown colour and orangey-blonde ends.

It was time to find something easier to maintain. Shorter and less teenage paintbox.

The hairdresser suggested wavy, shoulder-length layers.

Lovely.

After two and a half hours in the salon chair, I emerged with shiny, chocolate-brown hair in chin-length layers and felt SO much better. That haircut had been long overdue. And I didn't even need to blow-dry it – I could just let it air-dry.

Perfect.

Lastly, I addressed my make-up.

I hadn't worn make-up for ages, except to daub Miss Selfridge 'neon blast!' on Lexi for fun face-painting. Everything in my make-up kit was either unsuitable for day wear or dry, crumbly and out of date.

That Va Va Voom mascara and blunt kohl eyeliner must have been at least five years old. And those 'of the moment' unusual-coloured eyeshadows from Primark – had I ever worn those?

I threw everything out and bought a very simple Clinique make-up set: one mascara, some sheer lip gel, a powder foundation and an eyeliner.

Minimal and stylish.

Quality over quantity.

This felt better.

Me, pictured here looking less hobo-like for one of my author photos. I hate having pictures taken. I either look smug or constipated.

Slowly but surely, I was finally growing up. More slowly than surely. But it was happening.

#23 LIE – YOU SHOULD NEVER BRIBE YOUR CHILDREN

So it was goodbye big city, hello country life.

Eventually.

The house sale, mortgage, etc. was absolutely not a straightforward process (it never is, is it?) but in the end these were minor irritations. (Solicitors are soooo sloooow! Doing EVERYTHING by post. Get with the times, guys!)

We bought two huge dehumidifiers while we waited for solicitors to send a few letters back and forth at a snail's pace (very possibly by horse and cart).

The dehumidifiers made the air desert-dry and gave us itchy eyes and weird black snot, but at least the air wasn't damp and Lexi's chest seemed to be improving as we waited.

And waited.

When the house sale finally went through, Lexi was one and a half years old and fully able to unpack the boxes we'd already packed.

Being a toddler, she was also sensitive to criticism and threw a shit fit if we gently suggested she 'STOP UNPACKING THOSE BOXES,

FOR THE LOVE OF GOD! I'VE TOLD YOU A HUNDRED TIMES!'

After many hours of packing and repacking boxes, we finally got everything into the removal van and set off for our new home in the countryside.

We started early on moving day, with the movers arriving at 6 a.m., and had the keys to our new property by 8 a.m.

Once the boxes were unloaded, Demi and I ran around the property like lunatics, arms out and laughing at all the space.

Lexi imitated us, stumbling around on her little toddler legs and babbling, 'House, house!'

Perhaps we should have replaced those swirly pink carpets, wood-chip wallpaper and that dark 1970s kitchen before we moved in. Certainly, we should have removed those weird bathroom tiles featuring the semi-naked Grecian goddess. Definitely we should have taken out the 1970s gas fire with its faux flames.

But it was still a whole house, and we couldn't believe it was ours.

The owner had (very kindly) left Lexi a giant 1970s baby doll with sinister, unsmiling eyes, a grey face and a stained cloth body. Demi and I were terrified by it, but not Lexi. She loved that doll and immediately placed it in the largest bedroom.

'My 'oom!' Lexi declared.

'No, Lexi,' I said. 'That's Mummy and Daddy's 'oom. It's the biggest one with the nicest view.'

Lexi's smile faded. She locked eyes with me. 'My 'oom, Mummy.'

'No, Lexi. Your 'oom is this slightly darker, smaller one at the back of the house.'

'No, Mummy. This my 'oom.'

'Tell you what,' I bargained. 'How about Daddy and I have this room, and you have a strawberry yoghurt?'

'OK!' said Lexi, delighted.

The little fool.

I took Lexi downstairs for her strawberry-yoghurt bribe, but unfortunately I'd made an oversight. The spoons were packed away somewhere.

'Don't worry,' I told Lexi. 'We'll go out for a brunch-breakfast thing. A fun, treat breakfast. An adventure!'

I knew there was no McDonald's in this backwater village, but I was confident there would be some kind of cafe. Possibly a twee tea shop offering a fried breakfast with locally produced sausages.

Kids like sausages.

We left Demi to unpack and headed to the High Street (villages never really have high streets with real high-street shops on them – but, essentially, the place where the post office is), hoping to find a fresh chocolate croissant and perhaps even eggs Benedict for a special 'just moved house' breakfast.

We did not find these things.

There was only one cafe and it didn't do eggs Benedict. Only white-bread toast and scones.

And it was closed.

'OK, Lexi,' I said in my best 'I'm coping just fine, darling, and don't ask for that bedroom back!' voice. 'We'll have to resort to plan B. That little newsagents over there. I'm sure it will sell a sausage roll or similar treat.'

The newsagents sold four things: newspapers, chocolate, crisps and (rather obscurely) sticks of rock.

Lexi was hungry. I was hungry.

It started to rain.

Everything was starting to feel ominous, like maybe moving here was a very big mistake.

I went a bit mad and let Lexi choose whatever crisps and chocolate she wanted for breakfast.

'Breakfast?' Lexi asked incredulously in a voice that suggested Mummy wasn't concentrating *again*.

The counter lady raised an eyebrow.

'Yes, yes!' I said gaily. 'A special day. Ah, ha ha ha! What have you picked there? Wotsits? Oh for the love of . . . Couldn't you at least pick one with something made from potatoes? And what's that? A solid-chocolate Twirl bar? Would you prefer something with peanuts?'

But the threat of that smaller, darker bedroom loomed large.

I bought Lexi packets of Wotsits, Skips and Chipsticks for breakfast, complemented with a Mars bar. I bought myself something similar.

We pushed on in the rain, heads bowed and stuffing our faces with bright-orange crisps, when I noticed something wonderful – a library. A lovely, bright, warm library, right on the High Street. Our salvation from the rain. AND it was open.

I've always liked libraries. You have to if you're a writer. It's the law.

The library had dark, tinted windows, but I was quite sure inside would be full of colourful books and bright cushions.

'Quick, Lexi,' I instructed, parking up the buggy next to the panoramic, twinkling black window. 'Eat your Wotsits. Eat your chocolate. Hurry up! Then we can get inside in the dry.'

I shovelled chocolate and bright-orange crisps into her mouth and mine.

Then we entered the library.

Inside was a large mother-and-toddler group sitting on bright cushions, holding colourful books for their children right by the tinted window. Just as I'd imagined.

They were all staring at us.

I realised the glass, which was opaque from the outside, was see-through from the inside.

These mothers had just witnessed me ramming crisps and chocolate into my child's face at speed with 'hurry up, hurry up!' motions at nine in the morning. And not even organic potato crisps. Wotsits and Skips.

I gave a tentative smile, suddenly aware of cheesy Wotsits powder all over our faces.

One of the women said, 'Would you like to join us? We're singing "Little Peter Rabbit Had a Fly Upon His Nose".'

Lexi clapped her Wotsits-stained hands together in delight.

'We've just moved house and we don't have cutlery,' I said obscurely, trying to wipe away orange cheese powder.

The kindly mum looked confused. 'It's OK,' she said. 'You don't need cutlery to sing.'

We joined the mums, and they were lovely – not once cross-examining me about our weird snack/breakfast/brunch arrangements.

Perhaps this house move wasn't such a bad decision after all. There was a lot of love here. And wasn't that missing in the city? Love?

Brighton had all the vegan restaurants, organic produce and frozen yoghurt we could ever want, but no one in the big city (apart from our friends, obviously) knew our names.

Within half an hour of living in this village, five women were smiling and talking to us. They knew our names AND our slovenly breakfast habits.

After a morning of nursery-rhyme favourites, Lexi and I headed back to our new home.

Demi had unpacked everything and put furniture in the right places. He'd found the cutlery and ordered takeaway pizza for lunch. He'd put a little polka-dot blanket over the sinister baby doll in an effort to soften its evil appearance.

We sat on the swirly pink carpet, ate pizza and talked about how things were changing. How things *had* changed. Who'd have thought? All of us, out in the countryside without a McDonald's. And yet we seemed to be enjoying ourselves.

(Demi: 'I didn't enjoy that lunchtime much actually, because Domino's sent pepperoni pizza instead of Mighty Meaty. Essentially, "mini meaty". It made me feel unloved and unimportant, but I'm over it now.')

Over the next few weeks, we enjoyed our big palace of a house and its many, many windows. We loved our big kitchen and garden. I'd got a new wardrobe and haircut and no longer looked like a hobo. However, city to countryside is a BIG change.

Metaphorically, we'd gone from a 3 a.m. boozy party to a nice cup of tea with grandma. A packed-out gig at Wembley to a lone child blowing notes through a recorder. Glastonbury to Glyndebourne.

Despite evidence to the contrary (i.e. our tired and haggard faces, 9 p.m. bedtime and new family home), we still saw ourselves as somewhat dynamic. Exciting. Like people in a Pepsi MAX advert, albeit slightly grumpier, less energetic versions.

Did we really fit into this sleepy family place with its mooing cows and three pubs – all of which closed at 11 p.m.?

We had doubts.

Take the shopping situation, for example.

A few weeks after the move, Demi and I decided to sit in the garden and drink wine. It had been a long day and Lexi had screamed a lot.

Demi popped to the local supermarket to pick up the usual fridge-fillers (deli snacks and alcohol) and came back white-faced.

'There's no guacamole,' he said. 'And they've *sold out* of hummus.'

There was worse to come.

'The single drinks fridge was broken,' said Demi. 'I've had to buy warm beer and Prosecco.'

This was appalling news.

'What kind of place sells warm Prosecco?' I demanded. 'We're not *animals*.'

Then there was the lack of coffee. The only place in the village selling coffee was the aforementioned little tea room that catered for the cake-and-sandwich retirement crowd. The coffee was all right but it certainly wasn't the freshly ground flat whites we craved.

And if we wanted a gluten-free lunch, well, forget it.

Things were unsettling for Lexi too. We'd arranged for my mum to look after her for one day a week, but that wasn't enough to keep the wheels of commerce turning in our house.

Lexi having a great time with Nana.

(Demi: 'Su's parents were and still are amazing with the kids. Absolutely amazing. Thank you, Don and Jean.')

Now Lexi was walking and talking and approaching two years of age, we felt she was ready for nursery. The local nursery looked lovely, with a big green garden, and wellies filled with flowers decorating the gate. Still, this was a big change. No more Italian childminder to feed her pasta. No more one-on-one childcare in a home environment.

Lexi clung to our legs and screamed on her first day at nursery.

'Want home,' she said. 'Want Herby.' (Herby was her funny toddler friend from Brighton who bit people.) 'Want Nana. Want Mummy.'

Next to the nice, cosy childminder's house, the nursery *did* feel large and foreboding. Full of chattering children. It all seemed a bit 'law of the jungle', 'survival of the fittest', 'grab the toy you want and fight off the other children'. But I really did feel Lexi was ready, and it was time for her to grow with this experience. Just like we were growing.

Still, Lexi had a very, very big cry and clung to us mightily.

The nursery staff assured me that children play their parents like fiddles, pulling on heartstrings to get what they want.

'She's picking up on your unease,' they said. 'Once you settle, she will too.'

And we *were* unsettled. Moving house isn't easy and this new place was totally different.

#24 LIE – THEY'RE HAPPIER WHEN THEY CAN RUN AROUND

Over the next six months, Lexi settled into nursery. She no longer screamed her head off at drop-off and seemed generally content, chattering about her new friends and the various craft activities that gave us piles of glittery, scribbly paper to recycle each week.

Our daughter was approaching the terrible twos, walking and talking.

And she wanted to walk *everywhere*.

People said this would make Lexi happier. This was not the case.

Trying to get Lexi places was now a nightmare. If I strapped her into the buggy, she'd buck like an angry bull, crying, twisting, wriggling and sometimes actually getting loose. Public transport was bad too. Within minutes on a bus or train, Lexi would be howling, 'Want off, want OFF!' and hitting the nice smiling old ladies who tried to comfort and distract her.

Walking with Lexi was extremely slow. We're talking hours to make a fifteen-minute journey.

It soon became clear something was missing. Something that would make our lives a whole lot easier.

Yes, we needed a family car.

In Brighton, we hadn't owned a car. All the shops were ten minutes away and, anyway, there was nowhere to park.

Here, miles away from the nearest McDonald's, a car would make life a lot easier. Also, Lexi was always very at peace in the back of cars. She'd doze off or babble some little song and there would be no twisting, wriggling or bucking.

Demi couldn't drive, but I was sure as we purchased our own family motor vehicle that he would become determined to learn.

(Demi: 'I still can't drive. Ha!')

Which car should we purchase? How sensible did we need to get?

The very thought of purchasing one of those shiny, solid mummobiles filled me with dread. Who needs a car that size? And why get something so serious-looking? Where's the fun?

When we lived in Brighton, only two of our friends owned cars – Stocky and Alex.

Stocky owned a beaten-up, circa-1980 Mini Metro that sometimes ran, sometimes didn't, and required a special technique to get it started (rubbing the key to warm it up). He'd inherited the car from his grandmother and it eventually cost him £50 to dispose of for scrap.

Alex owned a large, shiny Vauxhall Astra – a family saloon car with sensible features like half-opening windows and child locks. This car had been given to him by his father as a twenty-first birthday present.

We were all OK with Stocky's 'grandma' car. It was a beaten-up, unpretentious item that served a purpose: taking a twenty-something man, and possibly a few friends, to festivals, on short road trips, etc.

Alex, on the other hand, was teased mercilessly for his 'sensible old man' car. This large, expensive vehicle was beyond our understanding.

Why would you get a car that's so BIG? Doesn't it use more petrol? It's not as if you can fit more people in it. And why on earth would someone pay thousands for a car when you can get one that runs for a few hundred quid?

However, as parents, we now fully understood those big hulking family vehicles. We wanted safety. Stability. A decent-sized car that took up a formidable bit of road space and roared at other vehicles.

Those tiny rattling £250 go-kart cars I'd owned as a teenager? No way. What if we broke down with a child in the back? It would be a nightmare.

Pre-kids, I had chosen cars based on price and colour. Is it under £300? Excellent. Do you have it in red? I'll take it. The model? What's that? Is it different to the make? Does it matter?

Now we had new priorities.

Safety. Reliability. Wipe-clean seats.

I began googling family cars, focusing on safety and reliability.

The top brand?

Volvo.

Of course. The saddest, old man-est car of them all. Could we really do it? Could we be the people with a 1970s family home and a Volvo on the driveway? Didn't we have a rep to protect?

Luckily, it turned out image mattered less to us than the safety of our precious daughter.

(FYI – I'm not saying Demi and I were ever particularly image conscious. If you want proof of that, you can find hundreds of Facebook photos of me in pyjamas and looking rough. Or of Demi in 1980s-shell-suit Arsenal jackets. But the image of ourselves as youthful and fun? *That* image. We cared more about our daughter than that image.)

After my usual obsessive Google-searching, I found a second-hand Volvo that sat heavily on the road and almost certainly wouldn't shake when passing great big delivery trucks.

The car was on sale at a local car dealership, so Lexi and I took the bus there.

I took Lexi's car seat along, pleased at my forward planning. On reflection, it was a terrible way to get a good deal. I may as well have held up a sign saying, 'Hello! I need to buy a car today, otherwise I'll have to lug this car seat home on the bus.'

As we reached the car dealership, the sun glinted on the many shiny cars in the courtyard. The car dealer let me test-drive some vehicles and was kind enough not to laugh when I forgot how to use a clutch and gears.

A deal was struck: I would pay full price for the car and the dealer would sell it to me.

As I drove Lexi home, I felt at odds with this sensible family vehicle. But when we hit the motorway, something happened.

Look at this car go! It was so sturdy. So smooth on the road. Why, it hardly rattled at all. The breaks were effective to the point of paranoid. And best of all, Lexi was protected by side and front airbags.

Surely no harm could come to her in this big hunk of metal.

We pulled into our driveway and Lexi and I assessed our new vehicle.

'Like Grandad car,' said Lexi.

'Yes, it does look a bit like Grandad's car,' I admitted. 'But it's very safe. And look at all the space in the back. We can throw your buggy in there and a picnic basket. Probably your bike and scooter too. And a dog, for good measure. If your dad would let us get a dog.'

(Demi: 'WE'RE NOT GETTING A DOG!')

We ignored comments from our childless friends about becoming sad and old and boring and moving to the countryside with a Volvo and a garage full of gardening equipment.

I mean, they were right. But we ignored them anyway.

With a car on the driveway, it was time to turn our attention to the house.

Lexi would soon be having her second birthday and she wanted it at home. When offered alternative (better) suggestions for party locations, such as a nice church hall, the soft-play area or really *anywhere* but home, Lexi point-blank refused.

'Home party,' she said. 'Pisscess' (princess).

'What about something less gender-specific, like Lego or *Star Wars*?' I prompted. 'We didn't bring you up to be a sexist.'

'Pisscess,' Lexi insisted. 'Pink pisscess.' Then she sang a song about a pisscess falling down a hole. Or something.

'Feminism is about choice,' said Demi. 'Lexi, you can have whatever party you like. A pink princess party at home, it is!'

'But we haven't redecorated yet.'

'We don't need to redecorate!'

'We do need to. We always said we would at some point. Wouldn't it be nice to have everything looking modern for Lexi's first big party with friends? We didn't do anything for her when she was one – just invited all our own friends over, ate cake and drank fizzy booze.'

When Demi and I moved into our house, we had been quite accepting of the 1970s, Joan Collins, old-lady den feel. OK, it wasn't our taste, but everything was gloriously maintained and had a cosy, retro orange-and-brown quality. Still, I always knew we'd make changes at some point and make the home really ours.

Remember those walls I told the former owner we wouldn't knock down? They needed knocking down. We had to get open-plan on this mother. No more small rooms. Modern Californian open space was the thing – especially if we were having a kids' birthday party with twenty toddlers running around in pink princess dresses.

'Please don't try and redecorate the house in two months flat,' said Demi. 'That sounds very, very stressful. What if it's not ready by the party?'

'It will be,' I said, one eye twitching. 'This is just the deadline we need.'

Of course, changing the house in time for Lexi's second birthday party would be a lot of work. But surely we were resigned to that now? Life with kids *is* hard work. It just *is*. I'd stopped expecting things to get easier months ago.

On my insistence, we began visiting hardware stores at weekends.

I sold these to Demi as fun, family outings. Trips Lexi would thoroughly enjoy (and actually she did, although this was a lucky guess on my part).

We deliberated over paint colours and finishes while Lexi shouted 'Pink, pink!' and held up totally unsuitable colours. We became those people: the ones obsessed with floor laminate and tiling suppliers and kitchen cupboards. The ones who know about hessian-backed, wool-loop carpet and costs/durability thereof. The ones who understand what a 'remortgage' is.

Even once we'd *finally* settled on a shade of chalky off-white for our walls (much to Lexi's dismay), Demi was still renovation-resistant.

Our house reminded him of his nan, he said, and he loved his nan. He believed 'if it ain't broke, don't fix it'. Didn't I know this about him by now? And while we were on the subject, he *hated* raisins and yet I regularly bought and offered him Cadbury Fruit & Nut chocolate. Didn't I know him at all?

I pointed out that the house was sort of broken. Being from a completely different century, it didn't fit this day and age. There was only one electric plug socket per room, no USB ports and an old fridge and dishwasher that burned through electricity.

'But what about all the noise and mess and disruption and stress?' said Demi. 'What if something goes wrong and the building work gets dragged out and our little angel's birthday party has to be *cancelled*? She'll never forgive us. She'll be psychologically scarred.'

'Nothing will go wrong,' I reassured him. 'People are always ripping out bits of their houses. It happens all the time. Probably it will just take a few weeks.'

'What about fitting the kitchen?' Demi asked.

'Probably just a morning,' I improvised. 'It's just hanging cupboards.'

I was sure – with our complete absence of building experience, coupled with no practical knowledge of houses – we'd have no problems whatsoever.

First on the agenda was ripping out the dated old brown kitchen and putting in a new one.

I was told by a number of sources that the 'ripping out' part was definitely something we could do ourselves, and not to bother wasting money on a skilled professional.

It was only demolition, after all.

Demi and I duly invested in a sledgehammer and a skip.

Lexi was hugely excited by these objects of destruction and kept trying to pick up the sledgehammer and hit things with it. She did an admirable job of lifting it clean off the floor before we launched across the room to stop her smashing the Lego.

Clearly, Lexi could not be around when we demolished things. She was finding it all far too exciting. Demi and I packed her off to her grandparents for the day and got on with the smashing all by ourselves.

With Lexi safely away from smashy-uppyness, we took a few tentative sledgehammer swings at the kitchen.

It didn't take long to discover that 1970s kitchens are extremely well made. We're talking solid wood here, none of your chipboard. It was a crying shame, actually, to take apart something so well constructed. But we'd already put a sledgehammer through the wine rack, so there was no going back.

After three hours of hitting and smashing, the kitchen looked very much the same. You could certainly prepare a spam sandwich or some pineapple and cheese on a cocktail stick if you were so inclined.

'We have to get this finished today,' I told Demi. 'The plasterer is due in tomorrow to do the walls. He said he would be booked up until Christmas after that. We can't have a building site for Lexi's birthday party. She'll never forgive us. She'll be psychologically scarred. You were right. You're always right. Why didn't I listen?'

Demi experimentally hit the breakfast bar with the sledgehammer, making a manly 'ARRRG!' noise.

The sledgehammer bounced.

'This kitchen is *unbreakable*,' Demi decided. 'We need industrial tools.'

We began to panic.

We did not have industrial tools.

'What about your dad?' Demi asked. 'He's got everything.'

True.

My dad is a massive hoarder. I asked Dad randomly, one Halloween, if he had a cast-iron witch's cauldron we could borrow. 'Yes,' he said. 'Do you want small, medium or large? And while you're at it, do you need a complete Roman soldier's outfit and/or Tudor gentry gear complete with sword for fancy dress? I've got both.'

'That's a good idea,' I told Demi. 'Dad knows about breaking things. He once destroyed an unbreakable car aerial by tugging it vigorously back and forth every time he got out of the car to prove its durability.'

I gave Dad a call.

'Lexi's fine,' said Dad defensively. 'She's only had one small bite of seventy per cent dark chocolate and the corner of a lemon meringue pie. And one or two bits of marzipan fruit. Maybe three. Don't go on at me about sugar – she's hardly had any.'

'We can't smash the kitchen,' I said. 'What should we do? The plasterers are booked tomorrow and if they don't come we won't be able to book them again until after Christmas and we'll have a toddler running around a building site and it will be awful.'

'What tools have you got?' Dad asked.

'A really big sledgehammer,' I replied.

'Where did you get it from, B&Q?'

'Ye-es.'

'They only sell toy tools there,' said Dad. 'I've got some proper industrial tools. I'll bring them over.'

Half an hour later, he turned up with two petrol-fuelled chainsaws and a six-foot sledgehammer. He called these tools 'the persuaders'.

By the end of the day, the kitchen lay in splinters at our feet.

'You want to get in touch with whoever put this kitchen in,' said Dad. 'And get them to put in your next one. They did a great job. Very solid.'

We began filling the skip with splinters of 1970s orange-varnished teak.

As I was throwing the last cabinet door into the skip, the elderly former owner walked past with her dog.

I tried to hide behind the skip, but she saw me.

'Hello,' she called out cheerily. 'Having a bit of a clear-out, are you?'

'Yes!' I replied, trying to push one of her cabinet doors deep into the skip and out of view. 'Just getting rid of some bits and bobs.'

'Righty-o,' she said, chuckling. 'Give me a shout if you want any advice about the best use of the kitchen cupboards. I always kept baking goods in the tall cupboard by the oven. They fit very well there and keep dry.'

'Yes, thanks!' I said, neglecting to tell her that the tall cupboard was now in the skip. As was the oven. 'Bye!'

The next day, the plasterers came to cover over all the 1970s wedding-cake-icing plaster with modern smooth stuff.

Lexi was back by then, and it was a nightmare keeping her out of the smashed-out hole of a kitchen. She was fascinated by it and kept toddling over to eat grit from the floor or sing sad songs about princesses with broken houses.

'Don't worry, Lexi,' I assured her. 'We'll have a nice new kitchen in a few days. Then we can stop eating Coco Pops and have a nice boiled egg and soldiers for breakfast. Look – here's the builder coming now to get started.'

'Bob the Builder,' came Lexi's excited response. 'Yes we CAN!'

'No, we can't,' said the builder. 'There's a big problem.'

If you've ever renovated a kitchen (especially if you want things to move quickly because you're sick of washing up in the bathroom sink and throwing half-eaten bowls of Coco Pops down the toilet and you're having a party for your daughter in a few weeks), you'll know there are always problems.

'The plaster is still damp,' said the builder. 'We can't fit a kitchen on damp plaster. You should have booked us in a few days after the plastering was done. Plaster always takes a few days to dry – especially in the winter.'

Apparently, everyone knows this.

'So what will happen?' I asked.

'You'll have to tape off that dangerous concrete area where your kitchen used to be. Stop the little one getting to it. We'll be back in a few months – we're booked up until after Christmas now.'

'Do you know anyone else who could fit us in this week?' I asked.

He shook his head. 'Not at this time of year. People want things finished before Christmas. Make a nice family home for the festive season.' He eyed up the stained, concrete shell that used to be our kitchen.

I did what any mother of a small child would do when faced with no kitchen and twenty toddlers coming for a party in a few weeks' time.

I cried.

We'd been living with a huge, concrete hole instead of a kitchen for days now. All our foodstuffs were stacked up in the living room, we had no fridge or oven and I was totally sick of seeing Coco Pops floating in the toilet.

Lexi kept escaping into the concrete hole that used to be the kitchen and stroking the oil-stained floor.

'Lexi, we might have to rearrange your party . . .' Demi began.

'Forget Lexi's birthday party,' I told Demi. 'If the kitchen isn't going to be done until after Christmas, what are we going to do on Christmas Day?'

'Eat Bernard Matthews turkey slices while sat on a roll of kitchen lino?' Demi suggested.

I raged about him being unsupportive. He raged back that he'd warned me about potential issues and that relationships were a compromise, not me just charging ahead and doing whatever I wanted.

As we were shouting at each other, my dad popped round with three Italian cream desserts he'd picked up at the cash and carry.

'That plaster looks a bit damp,' Dad pointed out. 'You'll need to get some industrial-sized heaters on that pronto or they won't be able to fit your kitchen.'

'Industrial heaters? Is there such a thing?'

'I've got three in the lock-up,' said Dad. 'I'll bring them over. They'll dry your kitchen out in no time.'

Half an hour later, Dad lugged three wardrobe-sized heaters into our concrete shell of a kitchen. They turned our home into the sunny streets of Italy, glowing blindingly bright orange.

Lexi put on the little flamenco dancing outfit Grandad had bought her in Spain and danced around in the mock sunshine, singing 'We're all off to sunny Spain – olé!'

Soon all the walls were bone dry and I was fairly sure we'd all caught a suntan.

The builder returned and prodded the walls speculatively.

'Yep, they'll do,' he said. 'Let's get going.'

A few days later we had a gleaming white-wood kitchen complete with one of those fridges that dispenses water and ice cubes.

The yellow floor lino was now solid wood and the wedding-cake plaster had been smoothed over.

There was a breakfast bar.

A dividing wall had gone, creating a Californian-style open-plan living space, and we'd smashed out the patio-brick fire surround and replaced the gas fire with a wood-burning stove.

We'd done it.

We'd achieved the perfect kids' party venue – loads of space and a fridge freezer that chucked out ice cubes at any toddler who could reach the lever. AND in time for Lexi's pink princess birthday party. Now all we needed to do was buy a lot of pink bunting, pink plates, pink cakes and so forth.

Dad came to the rescue again with fifty metres of bright-pink bunting he had 'lying around', plus some glittery paper plates and a giant pink elephant statue for princesses to ride on. He also had some foil balloons with 'Pimm's' written on them, which we declined.

Lexi ran around the new space, clapping with delight. And it was safe for her to do so – she could eat off this new floor if she wished. It was perfectly hygienic.

The next Saturday afternoon, a horde of playful, chattering toddlers arrived in pink princess outfits. A few of the boys disrespected the dress code by coming as Spiderman, Superman, etc. but Lexi was gracious enough to let them in anyway.

We'd hung the house with yards of pink bunting, set the breakfast bar with a party spread of jam sandwiches, pink-wafer biscuits, pink lemonade, iced fancies and other sugary delights. Oh, and the obligatory tomatoes and carrot sticks. You have to put those out even though the kids never eat them.

Some of the parents stayed and we had pre-Christmas drinks (no, November isn't too soon) in the 'dining area' while the kids ran around screaming and generally having a good time. Excuse the 'dining area' quotation marks, but these things were still surreal to us.

A *dining* area. My goodness, we were grown up!

Nana wearing a strange pirate headdress and holding Lexi at her birthday party. Family house complete!

We chatted about home renovations and B&Q discounts while our sensible family car sat on the driveway.

It was so weird. I'd been talking about home renovations, for goodness' sake! What had become of me?

But actually, it was a lovely day.

#25 LIE – SECOND PREGNANCIES ARE MORE STRAIGHTFORWARD

With all these big changes going on, you'd have thought Demi and I would want less hard work, not more. But no. Once the kitchen was renovated, Demi and I decided to have another baby.

The conversation went something like this:

Me: 'We should have another baby.'

Demi: 'Why would we want to do something stupid like that? When I think of all the work involved with a newborn baby, I feel physically sick.'

Me: 'Lexi should have a brother or sister; otherwise she'll be selfish and spoiled. Time is ticking. If we leave it too long, they'll be too far apart in age to play with each other. And I'm not getting any younger. Neither are you.'

Demi: 'I AM getting younger.'

Me: 'No, you're not.'

Demi: 'I suppose we'd better get on with it, then.'

Me: 'Yes. Let's get it out of the way.'

I'll be totally honest – we didn't exactly *want* a second child (sorry, Laya). Not yet anyway. Maybe in ten years when Lexi was closer to leaving home.

I felt in no way ready for two children. Lexi had now hit the terrible twos and was breaking things I didn't even know could be broken, like plug sockets. When she wasn't moving carefully tidied-away things out of their tidied place to somewhere I would trip over them, she required attention. A lot of attention.

'Mummy, Mummy, Mummy!'

Adding to this chaos was surely a terrible idea. But at least this time we'd sort of know what we were doing. Or at the very least, we'd know our inadequacies.

We started 'trying' for another baby, i.e. having fairly clinical but regular sex whenever we could summon the energy. After the first month, I took a pregnancy test and it came back negative.

This was good news because it was Demi's brother's wedding that weekend. Not being pregnant meant I could drink alcohol at the wedding – a last 'hurrah' to our former life, before we completely buried ourselves in children.

Excellent.

The wedding was fun, but drinking all day wasn't as fun as I thought it would be. Lexi was with my parents and we missed her terribly. Being without her . . . well, it just didn't feel right.

The next day, I felt awful. This was to be expected. I'd started drinking at 11 a.m. and carried on through until 11 p.m. But there was something *different* about this hangover. And also, something worryingly familiar.

Like morning sickness.

I took another pregnancy test, just to be on the safe side, but it still came back negative.

Still, I couldn't shake the feeling that I might be with child. We got pregnant really quickly last time. The first month of trying, actually. Bang! Back of the net.

The next week, I felt really tired and weird. One night, I gave Lexi cereal for dinner and fell asleep at 8 p.m.

This was worryingly familiar.

Surely I couldn't be *pregnant*? I'd taken two tests, for goodness' sake.

'I don't want to buy yet another £10 pregnancy test,' I told Demi. 'That's money I could spend on breakfast cereal for Lexi's dinner.'

'Do one more,' he said. 'Just in case.'

I duly bought the cheapest, crappest test in the supermarket – essentially a strip of cardboard in a box and the only test without a security tag on it.

I weed on the cardboard.

The cardboard said I was pregnant.

I phoned Demi in a panic.

'What have I done?' I shrieked. 'I drank shit loads of alcohol at your brother's wedding and we're PREGNANT. I've affected our baby's health for life.'

Demi calmly told me to stop being so ridiculous.

'The pregnancy test was negative after you drank all those shots,' he said. 'So you couldn't have done the baby any harm.'

'Yes, but I took the test too soon,' I said. 'I must have been pregnant the whole time. My period was five weeks ago.'

In my panic, I phoned NHS Direct and told them I'd poisoned my unborn child.

A kindly doctor came on the line. 'Congratulations!' he said.

'No,' I said. 'Not congratulations. I drank at least two whole bottles of wine last Saturday, and god knows how many shots.'

After a short, concerned silence from the doctor, I added, 'It was a wedding.'

'Oh!' said the doctor, clearly relieved. 'And when did you get the positive test result?'

'Today,' I said. 'But it was negative a few days ago. Those expensive digital "predictor" tests are bullshit.'

'You're fine,' the doctor assured me. 'The baby doesn't attach itself to the uterus for a good few weeks. The alcohol couldn't have affected anything yet. But don't drink from now on, OK?'

It was the best scientific explanation I had ever been given for anything.

I was flooded with relief.

Thank goodness. My slatternly ways hadn't affected my unborn child.

But then another reality hit home.

Shit, we were pregnant. PREGNANT.

Later THIS YEAR we would have *two* children.

TWO!

How on earth would we manage?

We would have a crying newborn AND a toddler running around.

Holy crap.

Not only that, but I would be pregnant for nine months WITH A TODDLER. (I don't mean I'd gestate a toddler, obviously. Excuse that sloppy grammar. No, I mean my pregnancy would exist alongside a toddler.)

I would be tired and throwing up while a little kid said, 'Mummy, Mummy, Mummy!' and threw things in my path to trip me up.

My first pregnancy was no picnic. I know some women love being with child, but I wasn't one of them.

'It's OK,' the midwife assured me. 'Second pregnancies are much more straightforward.'

Bullshit.

Second time around, I got every pregnancy symptom in the book and a few more nobody had heard of. I had twenty-four-hour morning sickness for five months, indigestion, haemorrhoids, anaemia, sciatica, headaches and some weird red rash on my foot, which the doctor had to look up under the 'rare skin conditions' section (and still couldn't find a name for).

As the pregnancy progressed, my anxiety grew. Partly, I think, it was due to wine deficiency. Since Lexi had stopped breastfeeding, I'd fallen right back into the bad habit of using alcohol to ease my worries. Now I had no such luxury. Only my own anxious brain, and there were a LOT of thoughts in there.

How will I look after Lexi while breastfeeding a newborn every few hours?

Will Lexi be jealous?

Will I be able to work and earn enough money?

What about morning sickness – will Lexi be upset that I'm too tired to play with her? Possibly scarred for life?

SHIT! Will Lexi wake up when the baby cries? She'll be so tired!

'We'll be fine,' said Demi. 'People all over the world have two kids. Some have three or four.'

This did nothing to reassure me.

FOUR kids! Oh good god!

'But I'm already not coping,' I told Demi. 'The low standards I've set myself such as "Don't feed your kid cereal for dinner" have slipped. I'm sick and only eating oven chips, breakfast cereal and Heinz tomato soup. And if I can't drink wine, HOW will I stop worrying about all this stuff?'

Soon, my anxious thoughts reached fever pitch.

Was I getting enough nutrients? Was I neglecting Lexi by lying around on the sofa, feeling sick and going 'ARRRG' with one cool palm on my forehead? Was it OK to give Lexi oven chips for dinner so often?

From Lexi's point of view, life was improving. The oven-chip, frozen-pizza and fish-finger ratio now far exceeded the freshly pre-pared vegetables, and she was getting to watch a LOT of kids' TV. But no mother wants an oven-ready, TV-heavy life for their toddler.

I thought I was over this anxiety stuff. We had a kid already. I knew the drill: lots of discomfort, pain, etc. There was no mysterious, unknown future to worry about. But as the pregnancy progressed, my anxiety came flooding back.

Anxiety II: Revenge of the Anxiety.

I was in for a whole ocean of it, wave after wave, knocking me over.

My brain ran riot, imagining danger at every turn, then planning for ways to mediate that danger with obsessive thoughts like: 'I need to clean the garage door RIGHT NOW because I won't have time when the new baby comes.'

Demi was always lovely and supportive, indulging my nonsense with kindness and offers of calming fruit tea. He looked after Lexi whenever he wasn't working, made all our breakfasts, did all the washing (he's always done that – he thinks I'm incompetent at it and I'm not about to correct him), got up in the night when Lexi cried, the whole lot.

He was awesome. I must have driven him mad.

One of the things I put my obsessive, manic brain to was getting lots of 'big tasks' done before the birth. This included house repairs, work projects and a really big one: Lexi *definitely* needed potty training *before* the new baby came along.

Why hadn't I considered this earlier?

I immediately googled potty-training tips and purchased the suggested 'equipment', which included:

- A star chart
- Two potties (one for upstairs, one for downstairs)
- A travel potty (no point explaining that one, is there? Oh, OK then. It's for travelling)
- Clip-on 'little kid' toilet seats
- A step for each toilet

I began the process of forcing Lexi to sit on the potty for ten minutes at a time, then administering stars for every tiny drop of urine she did on the shiny plastic.

> *(Demi: 'I helped with this too, just in case anyone thinks I was an absent, deadbeat dad. I came up with the great idea of letting Lexi watch* Peppa Pig *on the potty. Then Su shouted at me for "cheating", when in fact I was a free-thinking genius.')*

To Lexi's credit, she got the pooing straight away. But the weeing was a different story.

Potty Training for Control Freaks guaranteed Lexi would be fully continent within two days.

This did not happen.

What did happen? A lot of wee all over the floor.

'Do it in summer,' my mum urged. 'Then Lexi can run around naked and wee in the garden.'

'But I'll be really pregnant by then,' I said. 'What if we get behind schedule and Lexi isn't potty-trained by the time the new baby comes? What if we have to potty-train her when we have a newborn?'

I believe my breathing got rather frantic and Mum may have offered me a paper bag to take deep breaths into.

Eventually, after a few months of meltdowns and possible emotional scarring, Lexi finally peed in the potty. So I could stop worrying. Right?

Wrong.

It turns out anxiety doesn't work that way. You get one thing solved, then pop! Something else jumps up to fill the void. I had plenty more anxious thoughts in the bank to tide me over.

The next big topic for anxious consideration was sibling rivalry.

How would Lexi feel when I was breastfeeding the new baby and couldn't read her that *Meg and Mog* book over and over again?

What about the new baby crying at night – would Lexi miss sleep and get grumpy?

Would it bother Lexi that all her old clothes, bottles and soft toys were now in the nursery room, being dribbled and defecated on by another human being?

How would Lexi deal with Demi's and my lack of patience/reasonableness/understanding when we had a newborn screaming in our ears?

'You're already tired and grumpy,' Demi pointed out. 'Since you've been pregnant, you snap at everyone and go to bed at 7 p.m. Lexi's used to it. We all are.'

'You're tired and grumpy too,' I raged. 'Remember that doorstep incident? When you shouted at that British National Party candidate?'

'I didn't shout. I politely pointed out that he was an arsehole.'

But there was truth in Demi's accusations. Lexi was used to a grumpy, tired mother. Also, pregnancy had given her a good dose of 'Mummy lies on the sofa and goes "ARRRG"'. But linking that bad behaviour to another little human being – well, of course she'd be jealous, wouldn't she? I mean, she had two whole parents to herself. Soon she'd have half a parent at best.

I put these concerns to my dad, who dismissed them with a simple, 'Oh shut up, love. It'll be fine.'

But I *was* worried. So, so worried.

I asked friends with two kids how things had been, and mostly they confirmed jealousy issues – some with horrendously violent stories about small children whacking each other with sandcastle buckets.

I began obsessively researching ways to reduce sibling rivalry.

One child expert urged that the first meeting between first child and new baby be carefully planned to minimise hostility. Apparently, I must under no circumstances HOLD the new baby when Lexi meets it for the first time. We must put the new baby in a cot or buggy, and present her to Lexi as a 'gift'.

I informed Demi of the 'baby as a gift' plan.

'When we bring the baby home,' I informed him, 'you keep Lexi in her bedroom. Then I'll sneak the baby into its room, and we'll bring Lexi in and say "Surprise!" It's very important Lexi doesn't see me CARRYING the new baby.'

'Won't she freak out to see a new baby appear in the room out of nowhere?' Demi asked. 'What if she thinks the house is haunted? That the weird, grey-faced baby doll has conjured up a malevolent-baby spirit friend?'

'No. Lexi won't think that. She'll love the surprise.'

'Right,' said Demi in a way that suggested tolerance of my control-freaky ways but also a quiet understanding that all of this may not come to pass.

'Otherwise she'll be jealous,' I explained. 'And threatened.'

'Why would she be?' Demi asked. 'I was never jealous of my brothers. I just wanted to look after them.'

'But you're much nicer than I am,' I said. 'My sister and I used to throw each other through windows.'

'Were you jealous of your sister?' he asked.

'Not at all,' I said. 'She was my best friend. I mean, we fought but it was good-natured. We had sporting rules like no hitting faces or spitting.'

'Maybe you're just worrying yourself over nothing,' said Demi. 'You do that quite a lot.'

Cue hormonal pregnant explosion.

'One of us has to plan ahead!' I ranted. 'If we had it your way, we'd still be living in that damp flat in Brighton. AND you own twenty different shirts that are all exactly the same. Why do you need so many shirts? WHY? And another thing – why have you put house stuff in the *garden* shed?'

'What house stuff?'

'CHAIRS! And a box of wine glasses. They're HOUSE things. Why did you put them in the SHED?'

The nice thing about being pregnant is that being angry and mental is seen as normal. People just let you get on with it while quietly pitying you and your terrible haemorrhoids and flatulence.

#26 LIE – YOU SHOULDN'T FLY DURING THE THIRD TRIMESTER

As the second birth approached, my anxiety showed no signs of abating.

Demi suggested a holiday – one last trip away before the newborn nightmare hit us like five sack loads of extra washing.

'But they say you shouldn't fly during the last trimester,' I said. 'In case the baby comes early.'

'Our baby won't come early,' said Demi. 'You were really overdue, remember?'

'I WASN'T OVERDUE! THERE IS NO SUCH THING AS OVERDUE! THE DUE DATE WAS FORCED UPON ME BY THE MEDICAL PROFESSION AND I WAS PERFECTLY ON TIME FOR MY BODY.'

'You'll feel much less manic and crazy if we have a break,' said Demi. 'Travel will take your mind off things. We've only been away once since Lexi was born. And that holiday was awful.'

It was true. When Lexi was one and a half, we went on an ill-advised city break to Rome. We learned a valuable lesson on that holiday: hot, cosmopolitan cities and toddlers are a poor combination. Especially when mixed with gelato.

We spent that long weekend dragging an overheated, tired little girl from one tourist attraction to the next, supervising gelato-induced meltdowns and having panic attacks when mopeds shot out of alleyways and shop doorways.

Our evenings were spent sitting in a dark hotel room, curtains closed against the streaming Italian sunshine, whispering so as not to wake Lexi.

We could hear happy, laughing Italians on the street outside, enjoying their after-work Aperols and lengthy Italian meals. For some reason, we'd pictured ourselves doing just the same thing when we booked the holiday. We hadn't factored in the babysitting element. As I say, we hadn't grown up yet.

It was the classic novice-parent mistake – trying to have the sort of holiday we used to have, without appreciating that kids go to bed in a dark room at 7 p.m.

Italy is lovely, but you may as well be in Bognor Regis if all you see is the inside of a hotel room.

'Are you sure we should go away?' I asked Demi. 'It was fucking horrendous last time.'

'We didn't understand family life back then,' said Demi. 'We were thinking like non-baby people. Instead of looking for a cultural adventure, we need to do something easy. Child-friendly.'

'Won't that be boring?' I said.

'Excitement is tiring.'

We had a little cash to spare for a trip away. Moving house had cost quite a bit, but our new rural location was saving us a fortune in filter coffee, sushi, apple martinis and 'little trips' to the Tesco Metro for one more bottle of wine.

Also, our childcare financials had hugely improved. Mum looked after Lexi FOR FREE one whole day a week and sometimes babysat.

Additionally, Lexi was now two years old and had fifteen free childcare hours.

Thank you, government.

Thank you, wonderful parents.

A break before the chaos of a newborn hit sounded like a good idea. But where?

Pre-kids, we'd Interrailed around Europe, camped at boiling-hot Spanish festivals and windsurfed in Greece.

Exciting stuff.

However, the days of unencumbered, child-free travel were behind us.

Post-kids, taking a train around Europe sounded like a fucking nightmare. And windsurfing? Who had the energy? Our new buzzwords were 'relax' and 'unwind'.

We had a lengthy discussion about the sort of boring holidays people with children might enjoy.

'Why don't we get some of those family-holiday brochures?' Demi suggested. 'You know – the ones with the smiling, tanned family holding a beach ball.'

I considered this.

Did we want to be that bland, smiling, tanned family on a beach holiday devoid of culture and excitement? Had we changed so much?

To test the waters, I took Lexi into town and picked up a wodge of family-holiday brochures for Spain and Greece. They all had pictures of smiling, tanned families holding colourful beach balls on their front covers.

All of them.

'That tanned bikini woman isn't a real mother,' I told Lexi. 'She couldn't possibly be. Look at her perfect, flat stomach. Where are the wrinkly bits? The newly formed inside-out belly button? THAT bikini woman is holding a very young baby – clearly that child isn't hers or she'd have a weird brown line on her stomach.'

Aged two, Lexi didn't really understand. 'Not a mummy? *Is* a mummy, Mummy. She got baby, Mummy.'

On the train home, Lexi and I skimmed through the brochures.

The pictures looked nice. What was that – a cocktail bar *in* the swimming pool? And an all-inclusive buffet . . . whoa. So we wouldn't have to cook a single meal? No washing-up? Lexi could chuck stuff on the floor with gay abandon, safe in the knowledge that it was all bought and paid for?

Sign us up immediately!

Who knew holidays like this existed?

My childhood family holidays were self-catering camping trips, sometimes to the south of France if my parents were pushing the boat out. If we were lucky, my sister and I got a French baguette to chew on. If we were unlucky, we'd be carted to some wobbly meat restaurant and served something especially disgusting like liver in garlic butter.

An all-inclusive buffet was beyond luxury.

I decided this sort of extravagant holiday must cost a fortune. I mean, how much would a parent pay to have all their meals cooked for them and their child cared for at a kids' club? £10,000? More?

But apparently not.

Out of season, last-minute deals were pretty darned cheap. Around £200 per adult, including all flights, food and drink. Alcoholic drink.

This, we realised, was only marginally more expensive than living at home.

Why hadn't we discovered these 'package holidays' before?

We booked immediately and flew out a week later.

When we arrived in Corfu, it was better than OK. It was *lovely*.

The views were beautiful, the pools were sparkling clean, the food delicious and the drink plentiful.

Don't fly during the last trimester, indeed! What nonsense. A break was exactly what I needed.

Obviously I couldn't drink the alcohol, being pregnant. But everything was all so relaxing. It was great to do *nothing*. Truthfully, it was the first proper break we'd had since Lexi was born.

Demi and I kept giving each other obscure thumbs-up signs across the free bar.

£400 for all this! AND there was a kids' club.

We spent that week reclining on sun loungers, eating Greek pastries and watching Lexi splash in the toddler pool. Occasionally, we'd throw her an ice cream or a sugary drink. She was happy. We were happy.

We had *nothing* to do. Nothing! It was just brilliant.

By day three of the holiday, my anxiety had subsided. Maybe there was something in this 'taking things easy' lark. If I stopped running around at 100 mph and just lived life at a slower pace, things would be better.

Little Lexi enjoying her last days of freedom before a little sister is thrust upon her. Not sure what she's written in the sand. 'I love being an only child'?

I had something of a spiritual epiphany and started doing daily yoga and meditation. I downloaded Buddhist texts and tried to live in the moment, noticing the lovely little birds pecking up croissant crumbs outside the chow hall, and watching my precious daughter with soft, loving eyes as she stamped her feet and bellowed, 'No birdies! I stamp on you now!'

Buoyed up by this minor spiritual enlightenment, I began preaching Buddhist wisdom to little Lexi.

'Life is change, Lexi. Live in the moment. Breathe.'

On the last day of the holiday, Lexi lost a paper bag she'd decorated at the holiday club.

'I've lost my unicorn bag, Mummy,' Lexi screamed. 'I've lost it. MUMMY! Precious, Mummy! Need it, Mummy. Need to take it home, show Nana.'

There was no way I was walking around the baking-hot holiday resort, looking for an empty paper bag with a few childish scribbles on it.

'The Buddha says attachment is the route of all suffering, Lexi,' I told her calmly. 'That paper bag is just a thing. *You've* made it precious. But that's just a story. Loss is part of life. Move on.'

Lexi had what is known in childcare circles as a 'shit fit'.

She screamed and went red and shouted over and over again, 'I want my unicorn bag, I WANT MY UNICORN BAG!'

I tried again to explain about loss and attachment.

'It's just a thing. That's all. Let it go in your mind and you won't suffer any longer.'

'But . . . I . . . *loved* that bag,' Lexi stammered, through little choking sobs.

'It was just an empty bag,' I said again with a kind smile. 'You've attached yourself to something meaningless and you have to let go.'

'Not empty,' Lexi stammered. 'I put your jewellery inside.'

I sat bolt upright.

'What? WHAT? My jewellery was in it?'

Lexi nodded.

'MY jewellery!' I screeched. 'Where did you have it last? Where did you drop it? What are you sitting there for? We're going to find it right now.'

'Jewellery is just a thing,' said Demi, taking a sip of cold beer and reclining on his sun lounger. 'You've made it precious. Attachment is the route of suffering.'

'But I've had that lightning pendant since I was a teenager! It's irreplaceable!'

'That's just a story,' said Demi. 'Let it go.'

After I'd sworn a lot at Demi, I dragged Lexi around the resort for two hours, looking for the 'precious' paper bag. When we found it, all the jewellery was gone. God knows who took it – it was all cheap, costume stuff and fairly worthless to anyone but me. But Lexi was glad to find her bag again.

We came home relaxed and happy, eager to share our holiday experience with any poor sap who crossed our path.

'And it was only £200 a person! Although I lost a lightning pendant I'd had since I was a teenager . . . [sideways glance at Lexi] but life has loss, I've let it go . . .'

#27 LIE – SECOND BIRTHS ALWAYS HAPPEN QUICKLY

As labour approached, I considered our 'birthing plan' for baby number two.

Clearly, the first time around, things had gone terribly wrong. The induction. The emergency C-section. None of these things were nature's plan.

I made a bold and stupid decision – I would do everything within my power to have a natural birth.

People asked me why. If you're allowed to choose a C-section, why not do that? It sounds much easier. Lots of painkillers. And you've already got the scar. Plus, no offence, you seem like the sort of person who needs to know – to the minute – when the baby will come out . . .

I said I'd missed out on the miracle of labour and birth first time around and I wanted to experience what my body was designed to do: give birth. I wanted to connect with my inner mother.

Little did I know, my inner mother was a renegade. She didn't like pain or uncertainty and would in no way be giving birth naturally.

Sensible woman.

As the birth approached, I visited the midwife for the usual 'how would you like to give birth?' menu. I was offered either a C-section ('today's special', if you will) or a natural birth.

Foolishly, I decided to be a tough guy and try for a 'VBAC', which is not a type of bacon but a natural birth for women who have also had a C-section delivery.

'Are you sure?' the midwife asked. 'There's a chance of tearing your C-section scar, bleeding internally and dying.'

'How much of a chance?'

'One per cent.'

Mmm.

One in a hundred people might die. Quite high, really.

Still – I'm an optimist. My C-section scar looked pretty gnarly. Like a knotted rope, tough and durable. I was sure it wouldn't give up under pressure.

Let's go for it!

For some reason, I got it into my head that birth was an 'experience' I should have at least once in my lifetime.

I didn't consider that some experiences are awful. Prison, for example. Or watching pantomimes.

My sister, who by this time had given birth herself, told me that labour was like 'having boiling acid poured into your insides'.

'And I do make that distinction,' she said. 'It's *boiling* acid, not just normal acid.'

Foolishly, I ignored her.

As the birth approached, I stocked the freezer with ready-made lasagne and loaded the cupboards with high-quality hot chocolate.

I pulled Lexi's newborn clothes from the loft and worked out what we needed, having yet another panic attack over the newborn cowboy outfit that STILL had never been worn but was *so cute*.

I knew what was coming. I knew we'd have to batten down the hatches for a bit and that I'd probably shout at Demi for not doing things exactly as I did them. But I was pretty relaxed after the holiday and feeling ready to bring on the birth.

The due date came.

The due date went.

Fucking hell.

A week passed. I fielded the usual 'has the baby come yet?' phone calls.

Then finally something started to happen.

I got minor contractions every five minutes, all day long.

This was it! The big push! The natural birth on its way!

I meditated my way through the contractions. Stayed calm. Lived in the moment. Remembered my connection to mother earth and so forth. Burned joss sticks.

A sleepless night passed and I found myself still in labour.

How could this be? I'd missed a night's sleep, which was scary enough. But where was the baby? Was it stuck?

The pain was OK. Enough to make me leap up and walk around (which actually gets pretty torturous when you have to do it all day and night), but not agonising.

Another day and night passed.

This was bad.

I phoned my sister in a panic. She told me to calm down and stick on some romantic comedy.

I did.

The 1990s triple whammy of *When Harry Met Sally*, *Pretty Woman* and *Parenthood* saw me through another sleepless night.

The next day, I decided to go to the hospital, certain that the baby must be close to coming out.

They told me to go home – I wasn't in 'real labour' yet, and could be in this painful no man's land for days, if not weeks, to come.

Oh. My. God.

NOT REAL LABOUR?

No amount of meditation could quell my anxiety at this point.

I'd missed three nights' sleep. I mean, I had simply not slept. No sleep. Not even dozed a little bit.

People go mad from lack of sleep. It was a tactic used by Nazi guards.

I would go mad. I definitely couldn't look after Lexi if I'd gone mad. Plus, she would blame the new baby for my madness and no one would carry out my 'give baby as gift' plan and . . . ARRRG!

Why wouldn't this baby come out?

The labour-that-wasn't-really-labour lasted five days. Admittedly, I seem to add a day on every time I talk about my labour, so possibly it was four days. But it was AT LEAST three nights.

During these long days and nights, I'd pop into hospital every so often – only to be told to go home again.

The midwives and I developed a mutual hatred for one another. I saw them as evil Gestapo harpies, cruelly torturing a pregnant woman. They saw me as a massive drama queen.

During one journey to the hospital, I took a taxi, fidgeting in the seat every time a contraction washed over me.

> *(Demi: 'If you're wondering why my pregnant lady wife got a taxi by herself to and from hospital, you should know that she's highly independent and insisted she go alone while I look after Lexi at home. Also, I still can't drive.')*

'Have you ever been to Thailand?' the taxi driver asked me.

'YES!' I half-shouted as another contraction came along.

'Me too,' the driver enthused. 'Wonderful place, isn't it? I wrote some music about the sunsets out there.' He reached into his glove compartment. 'Do you want to hear it?'

'Sure,' I said, only half-listening.

'I'd better pull over,' the taxi driver decided. 'So I can find the right CD.'

He pulled over into a McDonald's drive-through and popped a CD into the stereo system.

'This is me, singing,' he said proudly. 'Not bad, is it?'

'I'm in labour!' I shouted. 'Why are you stopping the car? Drive to the hospital this instant. I'm about to have a baby!'

I got to the hospital, only to be told (again) that I wasn't actually in labour.

Some horrible quirk of fate meant I had the same taxi driver on the return journey home.

Life certainly has a sense of humour.

I spent the journey home listening to the taxi driver's faux rock voice singing about Thai sunsets.

Lexi was still awake when I got back and surprised to see me home.

'Baby not come out?' she queried.

'The baby won't come out,' I said, holding back a sob of panic. 'It won't come out!'

And it wouldn't.

I think my brain just wouldn't allow my body to let go. It was the anxiety. My body thought I was in danger and held on for dear life.

Finally, after repeatedly begging for a C-section, the hospital relented. But not before pointing out that they'd *offered* me a C-section *ages* ago and I'd turned it down.

'You should have made up your mind before labour,' said the midwife. 'We've had to pull a lot of strings to fit you in.'

I was too grateful to be rude to her. And far too tired.

The surgeon came to see me and said all the usual things: 'This is going to feel like washing-up in your tummy!'

And then, in a lower, more serious voice: 'Please sign this contract saying you might die during the procedure . . .'

After so many days of pain and missed sleep, I was delighted to see the lovely, civilised operating theatre and have the 'washing-up' sensations. Then little baby Laya was pulled out, covered in scabby blood.

Aww . . . birth is magic.

Then I was rolled to the labour ward, holding just-born baby Laya. Demi was waiting there with Lexi.

I had a moment of panic.

'We need to enact the "baby-as-gift, no-jealousy" plan!' I shouted at Demi.

'Just worry about healing from the C-section,' said Demi. 'Lexi wants to see her little sister.'

We showed Lexi the new baby, who was sleeping on my chest.

In her childlike, toddler language, Lexi said something like: 'Where's the chocolate? You said there'd be chocolate here.'

She wasn't jealous of the new baby at all. Simply gloriously indifferent in that selfish way toddlers are.

What a relief.

I told Lexi that the new baby was called Laya. Like the princess in *Star Wars*.

Lexi asked again about chocolate.

I worried Lexi would be upset about me being in hospital, but she was getting loads of attention from Nana and Grandad. Her sobbing, anxious mess of a mother was not a necessity.

Things were OK.

After a few nights in hospital, during which I met a woman who had a fourteen-pound baby that needed two doctors to lift it out, Laya and I were driven home by – yes, you've guessed it – the same Thai-sunset taxi driver.

That was a long journey.

#28 LIE – TWO KIDS ARE THE SAME WORK AS HAVING ONE

Home at last and so it began – another cycle of newborn nurturing.

We should have cracked this baby business by now, but there were more lessons to learn before we reached the holy grail of family happiness.

Exhaustion, recovery from a major operation, morphine withdrawal (I'm not an addict!), baby blues, an energetic toddler AND a newborn baby made me a physical and emotional wreck.

I was so, so anxious for the first month that I barely slept.

Bloody hormones again.

I just wasn't myself. I snapped at Demi over everything (he might say this is exactly like myself, but he is wrong – like he is about everything . . .). I cried for no reason. I kept going on and on about how I couldn't do this. I felt totally overwhelmed.

When I wasn't panicking about the near future, there was the long-term future to worry about.

How on EARTH was I going to work when my brain had stopped functioning? I was so much dumber than when I'd had Lexi. Post-Laya, people's names escaped me. People I'd known all my life.

Laya grew up learning that 'Umm . . . Errr' were common enough vocabulary words to use on a regular basis. 'Umm . . . Mummy, errr . . . need a wee.'

If I couldn't think, I couldn't work and I couldn't earn money and Laya just woke up again and ARRRG! WE ARE ALL GOING TO DIE!

If I'd bothered to slow down for a minute and connect with reality (nobody is dying and I hadn't gone *that* mad from lack of sleep), I would have seen that everything was fine.

Better than fine. My parents were around to help out. Demi was lovely. The kids were healthy. We had a family home and a mould-free shower. A very safe family car. We knew how to fit the child seats and fold up the buggy in a matter of seconds.

Still, anxiety gnawed at me day and night, and this time I couldn't escape into a world of cheery Christmas rom-com with a sleeping baby on my stomach. Childcare was now twenty-four hours a day, seven days a week.

Before I had Laya, people said two kids were easy. 'You've already got the equipment, so you just sort of slot them in. It's no more work than one.'

For me, it felt like a LOT more work.

I fed Laya every two and a half hours. I changed her. I rocked her and put her to sleep. I did humiliating breast-pumping on my sore boobs. And in the brief moments she slept, I cared for a verbally abusive toddler who screamed because I wasn't paying attention to her latest scribbled masterpiece.

When Lexi was born, there were some OK moments. Usually – and no, I'm not trying to be funny – when she was asleep. I got to watch a lot of Christmas movies and eat chocolate cake.

With a toddler and a baby, you don't get chocolate cake. Or Christmas movies. Well, you might get the chocolate cake, but you have to stuff it into your mouth while your toddler isn't looking.

I could not sit and stare into space while the baby slept, idly considering all the washing-up I should do.

No.

Lexi demanded adoration all day. And three meals. And a bath. All this while feeding and jiggling a newborn every few hours.

With Lexi, I'd still clung to the last remnants of my old life – albeit with white knuckles. Demi and I had a meal out occasionally. I did yoga once a week. Sometimes, Lexi and I ventured out of the house together. I had a small degree of independence.

> *(Demi: 'I don't remember having meals out. Are you counting eating fish and chips, sitting on our pink carpet because we didn't have a dining table back then?')*

All that changed with baby number two. This was for real now. Parenting with a capital P. No turning back. Swim with the tide or drown.

My biggest struggle with Lexi had been feeling like I was doing a shit job.

This time around, I was fully accepting that I was doing a shit job. My struggle now was wanting a break from the shit job.

'You need to slow down,' said Demi. 'Take things easy. Accept you can't do as much. Get used to being at home. Enjoy it.'

'But I don't want to do that,' I said. 'That sounds really boring. I just need to get organised. Do some forward-planning. I'm sure if I work out the timings, I can take a newborn breastfeeding baby and a toddler into town and have a nice lunch somewhere.'

'Well, if you're sure . . .' said Demi uncertainly.

I decided not to drive the car into town because I couldn't drive and breastfeed Laya at the same time, and this would make timings extremely difficult.

A trip to town on the bus was planned.

Road trip!

At first, things seemed OK. Lexi left the house with two different shoes on and her pyjama bottoms, but she was dressed so I counted this as a victory. I breastfed Laya at the back of the bus, glaring at anyone who looked in our direction.

Then it all went horribly wrong.

I'd forgotten.

Toddlers take so *long* to walk anywhere.

With a newborn screaming to be fed, dragging a toddler to the nearest toilet is awful. So is sitting on a closed toilet seat with a toddler at your knees, urging a newborn baby to hurry up and feed.

On the way home, the bus driver wouldn't let us on the bus.

'I'm not set up for that,' he said, jabbing a thumb at the buggy. 'You'll have to wait for an accessible bus.'

'When's that due?' I asked.

'Could be three hours or more. Who can say? We've only got a couple of them on the route.'

'We need to get on this bus,' I insisted. 'For medical reasons.'

'What medical reasons?'

'I have to breastfeed in ten minutes. I'll fold the buggy up. It folds up.'

Ignoring the bus driver's protestations, I humped the buggy on to the bus, dragging Lexi behind me, and proceeded to empty the overly full buggy basket of wet wipes, spare clothes, boob cream, snacks, etc. on to the luggage rack.

Then I tried to fold the buggy, kicking the Maclaren folding mechanism like a motorbike pedal, until eventually it succumbed.

'You can't put that buggy on the rack,' said the driver. 'It's dangerous.'

'Not as dangerous as I'll be if you don't let us on this bus!'

He let us on.

I got home in tears, vowing never to leave the house again. But I really wanted to leave the house.

I began to sympathise with those 1950s women who took 'mother's little helpers' to see them through the boring days.

When Demi came home, I let it all out. How furious I felt about being trapped inside, not able to stretch my legs, getting fatter and fatter, not even being able to watch Christmas movies because I had a toddler running around saying 'Mummy, Mummy, Mummy!' and wrecking the place.

True, sometimes Lexi went to nursery and sometimes my parents took care of her. But most of the time she was home with me.

I didn't enjoy sitting on my big, fat arse, breastfeeding while trying to entertain a toddler.

I did not want to be this bovine, atrophying human body.

To stay inside *all day* – well, I hated it.

Demi, in his nice calm way, said, 'Maybe you're just trying to do things too fast. Taking the bus into town was too big a challenge. Why don't you try something easier? Tone down your expectations?'

It was unpleasant yet sensible advice.

'I want an extra-strong hot chocolate from Costa in a paper cup with whipped cream on top,' I sobbed. 'Is that too much to ask?'

'There's a Costa Coffee concession at the supermarket,' said Demi. 'Why don't you take the kids there in the car tomorrow and get yourself one of the Christmas-special hot chocolates? They're doing Black Forest gateau this year.'

A trip to the big supermarket? Hardly the adventure I craved. Still, Demi was usually right about things. Damn him.

The big supermarket wasn't as exciting as travelling around Thailand, but actually – well, it was a nice day out.

Supermarkets are geared up for mums and toddlers. Extra-large parking bays. Trolleys with space for two kids. A mother's feeding room. It's nice to feel loved and wanted.

If someone had told me, pre-kids, that I'd count going to the big supermarket as a 'day out', I'd have been mortified. Shit, what had happened to me?

But finally I was getting it.

I needed to change. Slow down. Let go of the past and embrace the new. And not care what the old independent me had to say on the matter.

Enjoy the supermarket. Live in the moment.

However, while this mega mind-shift was taking place, there was a final mountain to climb before we could settle into family happiness.

I was worried about money.

Our expenses had gone up again since Laya was born, but my working hours had been severely curtailed.

Before we had kids, Demi's brother had told us that having a baby was pretty much the same as keeping a cat, cost-wise. There were the wet-wipe expenses and the initial outlay on equipment (buggies and so forth). But he assured us they weren't the huge financial burden people imagined.

Did I mention Demi's brother only has one child?

One child can slot neatly into a two-bedroom apartment. Who needs to buy a house with a garden? If *one* child wants to play outside – well, let's get our coats and go to the park. No, not that coat. The other one. Why have you taken your socks off? For the love of . . . you *can* put them back on yourself. And why do you want to bring a bag full of stones with you? No, you don't need to drag that along . . .

By the time we had two kids, the financial needs of family life were hitting hard. We had a mortgage, that sensible family car, nursery bills and many, many pairs of shoes to buy (stop growing!). Birthday parties, Santa's grotto at Christmas, Easter-egg hunts, books, craft materials, repairing things your kids have damaged. It all adds up.

I felt worried.

We needed to make more money. Raise our game. Make sure our income matched our new family outgoings.

It was no longer OK simply to earn rent money and a few beer tokens. That didn't cut it with two dependants.

My first two novels had done OK, but I needed to hit the bestseller lists to make any kind of living, and that was exactly what I intended to do – write a bestseller. Ideally, many bestsellers.

'I need to get back to work,' I told Demi. 'Immediately. Or we're all going to die.'

'Don't you think you'll be a bit stressed if you do that?' Demi asked. 'Your eyelid is twitching. I'm looking at new jobs. Something with a stable wage and—'

'WHAT ELSE CAN I DO?' I yelled. 'Do you want our children to starve to death?'

'You're worrying about things that haven't happened yet,' said Demi.

'Well, someone has to!'

'Everyone worries about money when their kids are young,' said Demi. 'But it'll all be OK. Lexi will be at school in a few years and we'll have more time to work. Just be patient.'

'If I'm patient, we could starve!'

I came up with an elaborate childcare plan involving my parents, two-hour breastfeeding windows, a laptop and some headphones.

'No one's going to starve to death,' said Demi. 'We've got enough food in the kitchen cupboards to last at least six months.'

Admittedly, this was true. During my many healthy-diet experimentations, I'd bought weird and wonderful dried-food products and powders that had been tried once then pushed to the back of the kitchen cupboard.

I'd gone wheat-free for a while (rye flour, spelt flour and corn flour). But when those first batches of muffins and pancakes went horribly wrong, the dusty, wholesome flour packets were abandoned.

'Wouldn't you like *normal* pancakes that aren't burnt and don't have holes?' Demi had tactfully suggested.

I'd ignored him and gone full-on gluten-free.

'Coconut-flour and rice-flour pancakes this time! Let's see how this batch turns out!' They were even worse than the wheat-free ones. 'Coconutty sawdust' was Demi's description. 'Coconut omelette' was Lexi's.

It was true – we did have a lot of food in the cupboards and were unlikely to starve to death.

Still, I felt anxious.

Demi told me to calm down.

It's amazing how that never works.

Financial worry was hardwired into me and it wasn't going to just go away.

I should share a little of my family background at this stage.

My maternal and paternal grandparents all came from the sort of poverty-stricken, broken-down towns you see in Wild West movies. Bleak mining areas where half the houses and shops are boarded up, slack-jawed drunks weave along the pavements, and faded Lux soap packets blow on the breeze like tumbleweeds. No work and no prospects.

All my grandparents moved down south to work in factories – some of which gave them mild lead poisoning. They saved every penny and never wasted anything. My maternal grandfather could make a piece of chewing gum last all week. My paternal grandmother only used soap on a Friday.

My grandparents were *very* anxious about money because they'd known a life without it.

They passed this anxiety to my parents, who passed it on to me.

Essentially, none of this is my fault. Are you listening, Demi? This is inherited worry.

But knowing where your worry comes from does not make it feel less real. And we *had* experienced a huge income drop, coupled with more outgoings.

'This is just a temporary situation,' said Demi. 'I studied this phenomenon in Sociology. Before you have kids, your disposable income is high. Then, when you have young kids, your earnings drop to poverty level. And then when the kids go to school, your earnings go up again.'

'We're at POVERTY LEVEL?' I exploded. 'That sounds awful. We'll have to wear potato sacks and do our own dentistry. I won't let our family sink that low.'

I careered forwards with my crazy work-schedule plan, taking Lexi to nursery, breastfeeding Laya, passing Laya to my parents, then desperately trying to push my mushy brain into shape and get some work done. As soon as I got going, I'd have to get back into baby mode again and feed Laya. Or pick Lexi up from nursery. Or cook a child-friendly, healthy meal that wouldn't get eaten.

It was stressful.

'Things have changed,' said Demi. 'You can't work the way you used to. We've just got to accept how things are. Stop buying all those crazy gluten-free flours you don't eat. Forget about holidays for a while. We can repair our own boiler and roof.'

'How about we cancel your Sky Sports subscription?' I suggested.

'Why don't you stop buying all that expensive hot chocolate?'

'Fuck off!'

Things were getting serious.

We weren't playing at life any more – the kids had made sure of that. Somehow we had to make this work.

Demi applied for new, better, more stable jobs.

I bought an extra-strong brand of coffee called 'hair curler', got my head down and started writing.

There would be no more *Big Brother* episodes of an evening, not for a long while.

For the next couple of years, I would work harder than I'd ever worked before.

I would write like the wind, I tell you. The wind. And eventually it would all pay off.

#29 LIE – THEY GROW UP SO FAST

Childcare. Working. Childcare. Working. Occasionally a bit of sleep and a hot chocolate. More working and childcare.

After a long, difficult few years, Lexi was finally nearing school age. Laya was toddling around, wrecking stuff and voicing opinions.

Time hadn't 'flown by' as people claimed it would. Not in the slightest. Laya's first few years were possibly the longest of my life.

I wrote 6,000 words a day, working on blind faith that if I put in the hours I'd create a mega-bestselling manuscript.

When Demi wasn't working or looking after the kids, he applied for stable, well-paying employment.

We'd put the kids to bed at 7 p.m., then pull out our laptops and tippy-tap away until we were too tired to stay up any longer. Then we'd go to sleep and start all over again the next day.

The house was permanently a catastrophe – Laya was toddling around, talking nonsense and carefully moving tidied-away objects out of their designated places and on to the floor.

Laya pictured here after finding a jar of Sudocrem. You know something bad has happened when they go quiet.

Lexi was a proud big sister, telling Laya everything she knew whenever possible.

'Yes, Laya. Broom. Br-oom. For sweeping the floor, yeah? Tape measure. To measure us. We are grow-ing things. GROWING. Like you, yeah? You're growing.'

The kids were growing.

But very slowly.

I kept imagining the future, when the kids could dress themselves, go to the toilet by themselves, stop throwing food on the floor, etc. Life would be better then, right?

'When Lexi starts school,' I said, '*then* things will be easier. I'll have more time. When Laya is potty-trained and gets her free hours at nursery. When Laya stops eating the insect repellent and saying "Spicy, spicy!" *then* life will be better.'

I knew I should live in the moment. Enjoy this beautiful time. Focus on the positive. But I also knew that unless we pushed to the next level financially, life with two dependants would get tougher and tougher.

Before I had kids, I thought I was hardworking. After all, I'd get up at 6 a.m. to write 1,000 words and *then* do a full-time job. It's a hard, insecure life being a writer. But fun too. It has a certain romance, doesn't it? I get up at *6 a.m.* to write . . .

I'd worked hard all my life, but with two little kids this was a whole new level. After Lexi was born, I'd somehow managed to finish that second book for my two-book publishing deal. I did this through late nights, early mornings, stress and way too much wine.

Now we had *two* kids and no publishing deal. My existing publisher didn't buy my latest book (*The Ivy Lessons*, a romance between a teacher and a student with lots of sex scenes) and nor did any other publisher.

Shit.

I had not expected that.

I should have been disheartened and thrown the manuscript into the bin, but instead I felt a quiet determination bubble up inside me. Somehow I would get this book in front of readers and *they* could decide if the story was any good or not.

If readers hated the book – well, fine. But I thought it should have a chance.

Between working every hour I could, writing, and looking after the kids, I learned how to self-publish *The Ivy Lessons* and put it up for sale. In truth, I didn't really expect much to happen right away, and assumed I'd have to do lots and lots of social-media hawking to get sales going.

I was wrong.

Within weeks, the book totally caught fire and started selling thousands of copies. Within months it was selling tens of thousands, then hundreds of thousands.

This felt fantastic.

A real Cinderella story.

After years and years of struggle, rejection and being a 'poor but happy' writer, I was actually one of those overnight-success stories you hear about.

Me!

So there you go, anyone else who is struggling. The only way you can fail is by giving up. Keep going and you'll get there.

For the first time in my life, we had no money worries whatsoever.

Readers started emailing me, asking for new books. I wrote the Master of the House series, then decided to take a bit of a risk and write something different – a romantic comedy about motherhood called *The Bad Mother's Diary*. This would document all the amusing/distressing things about being a parent and put them in a nice romantic comedy for everyone to laugh at.

It was so different from what I'd written before that part of me expected it to sink like a stone. Still, worth a try. I knew *exactly* how much single-mother Juliette deserved her happy ending.

When I finished *The Bad Mother's Diary*, I knew it was a long shot. Everyone was saying romantic-comedy books weren't the thing these days. Over twenty publishers rejected the manuscript, which didn't surprise me. Publishing editors are usually youthful, stylish and child-free. They don't want to read about kids emptying Rice Krispies boxes on the bed or understand why weeing yourself as an adult is funny.

Once again, I self-published and stuff started happening. Great reviews appeared. Hundreds and hundreds of five-star reviews. (There were a few shit ones too, but let's gloss over those.) Then thousands of five-star reviews. Copies began flying off Amazon's virtual e-book shelf.

The book, I was told, was lifting people's mood, making them laugh out loud, making mothers feel loved and happy.

This was exactly why I had written it.

I was beyond proud.

Emails flooded in. Mothers told me how much they loved the book, how much they'd laughed, how they'd in fact *cried* with laughter and could I please write another one?

'Blimey,' I thought. 'I knew it all along. I AM a genius.'

That same week, Demi landed the job he'd been after, and we felt extremely lucky, happy and blessed.

After years of long, hard slog, things were finally coming together.

One fine spring morning, *The Bad Mother's Diary* hit the UK Kindle top five and I was beyond delighted. It was right up there with Stephen King's latest release.

Wow!

Demi was at work, but I was determined to celebrate in some small way.

'Kids,' I announced. 'We're going to the garden centre. We're going to buy a tree to commemorate this happy time in our lives.'

Lexi was nearly four and old enough to be excited by that sort of thing, and Laya was too small to complain.

'What sort of tree?' Lexi asked.

'Umm . . . a fruit tree.'

I said this in a confident and assured manner, hoping the kids wouldn't rumble my lack of gardening knowledge.

'That will take a *long* time to plant, Mummy,' said Lexi. 'Growing things. You need a *big* hole for a tree. The gardener at nursery said. Like a crater.'

'Oh, gardening is easy,' I said.

Off we went to the local garden centre in our sensible car. When we got there, the kids fought about who went in the trolley.

I made those unenforceable parenting threats you hope the kids never call your bluff on. You know the ones: 'I'm taking you home RIGHT NOW if you don't stop giving your sister Chinese burns.' Or: 'No more sweets EVER again if you don't put that down!'

We looked at fruit trees.

'What do you fancy, kids?' I said. 'How about a nice apple tree?'

A long, thin, elderly gardening assistant sidled up to us and said in a gentle voice: 'Not a great time to plant trees, actually. It's been an overly warm spring.'

Time of year? Was that a thing? Couldn't you just stick trees in the ground whenever?

I began turning tree labels over, casually looking at the growing instructions. Then I moved on to packets of vegetable seeds.

'WELL, Lexi and Laya. Of course, lettuce, as everyone knows, is very good to grow at this time of year . . .'

The gardening assistant leaned in again. 'Depends where you're growing it. Do you have covered veg beds? For the slugs?'

I abandoned my faux gardening knowledge and asked the assistant for help. He said, as Lexi had, that trees needed very big holes. Maybe I should just go for sunflower seeds.

'You can't go wrong with those,' said the assistant. 'They're idiot-proof.'

I'd have liked to tell the assistant that I wasn't an idiot, but actually, in the world of gardening, I am.

'We can grow these in the garden,' I told the kids, taking a sideways glance at the gardening assistant. 'And have big flowers in a few weeks' time.'

'Actually, growing takes time—'

'Come on, kids! We'd better get going.'

Back home, I made a big song and dance of planting the sunflower seeds.

'We'll grow one for each of you, girls,' I said. 'And for your dad and me. Then we'll have a sunflower family.'

'Will they grow by tomorrow, Mummy?' Lexi asked, eyeing the colourful seed packet with its bright yellow flowers.

'Not tomorrow,' I said in my wise parent voice. 'Maybe by the end of the week.'

But nature, it turns out, is lazy. And slow. Growing is a slow business. It happens little by little so you barely notice, and then one day – *poof!* Your kid is big enough to reach the top drawer in the bedroom, run downstairs with your condoms and post them through the neighbour's letterbox.

It was the same with my books. I wrote for years and years and then suddenly – *poof!* Just like that, things took off.

A week after seed-planting day, nothing was happening. Well, tiny little sprouts happened, but no sunny yellow petals.

This was crap.

I checked the seed packet.

'Oh, hang on,' I told Lexi. 'No, it'll take more than a week. THREE MONTHS! Oh, for goodness' sake.'

'How long is three months?' Lexi asked.

'Well. You'll nearly have started school by then.'

'Things take a long time to grow,' said Lexi in her wise-before-her-years child voice. 'Nature is patient.'

'Who told you that?'

'No one. I just knew.'

So we had to be patient. And with careful watering and nurturing, the sunflowers grew as tall as the kids.

Taller.

By the end of summer, our garden glowed with bright-yellow petals, and as the petals wilted we collected the seeds.

Now we have sunflowers in our garden every year – one for each member of the family. But it took a REALLY long time to grow those first seeds.

Fucking ages.

Natural things don't grow fast, with the possible exception of mould. But as I learned to be more patient, I enjoyed the growing much more.

#30 LIE – GIRLS DON'T FIGHT AS MUCH AS BOYS

As summer approached, I had three profound realisations.

First, I was enjoying being with the kids much more than I used to.

Second, Lexi would start school soon and be *really* grown up.

Third, Laya was excellent at fighting these days. We're talking proper kidney punches.

'NO, LAYA!'

This was the reigning cry in our house the summer before Lexi started school.

Second children are little firecrackers. They have to be. They need to take down someone much bigger than them, preferably immobilising them entirely so they can run for the hills before getting thumped with a big-sister fist.

Laya would knock her big sister over, then hide inside a kitchen cupboard or a suitcase to escape retribution. Sometimes Lexi would admit she deserved the violence. More often, Laya was a bit heavy-handed – thumping first and reasoning later.

At first, we admired Laya for tackling bigger children. How coura-
geous. Then she started biting people.

I'll admit, I'm partly to blame for this.

The first person Laya bit was an older boy at a birthday party. He
stole her cake, then held it high in the air and literally said, 'Nah nah
nah nah nah!'

Laya bit his arm.

The boy dropped the cake.

I thought it was quite funny. I mean, needs must. He was a really
big kid and the cake was the last pink Mr Kipling French Fancy.

Of course, I did the 'good parent' bit and told Laya not to bite, but
I think she picked up on my secret pride. She went on to bite kids her
own age who hadn't snatched her cake.

I realised my error.

No, Laya. Biting is never acceptable. No, never. OK, yes, if an adult
is trying to kidnap you, Lexi, yes, you're allowed to bite then. But by
and large, no.

As Lexi prepared for school, trying on her new school uniform and
writing her name on her school books (really she wrote an illegible X,
but we humoured her), sibling squabbles reached fever pitch.

We're talking hourly rumbles.

Laya wanted to do everything Lexi did and would bite and push
in protest.

It didn't matter that Laya was barely two years of age and incontinent. She wanted to write her name, and if that meant biting her sister
to get the pen then she would jolly well do so.

Lexi didn't help. She made tactless comments like, 'Your unicorns
look like dogs, Laya.' Or, 'You have baby legs.'

These thoughtless remarks would result in howls of rage, pushing,
shoving and sometimes acts of vandalism.

Then Lexi got a new school uniform. A pencil case. A school bag.
Shiny new shoes.

Laya wanted all of these things.

Demi suggested we get Laya her own school uniform so she could join in with her big sister.

I said that buying Laya things she didn't need would spoil her.

Demi said I'd bought the girls ridiculous Minnie Mouse Havaiana flip-flops when they already had sandals. They couldn't walk in those flip-flops – the Havaianas kept falling off. The girls certainly didn't *need* them.

I shouted that the flip-flops were on sale and a bargain.

We compromised. Laya wore one of Lexi's oversized school dresses.

The kids still fought.

Siblings fight. They all do it.

Girls, boys or gender-indeterminate.

(Demi: 'I rarely fought with my brothers. Violence and aggression come from your side of the family.')

However, as the fighting went on, we had an uncomfortable realisation.

Yes, the kids fought about kid things. Whether Pokémon were a type of ghost ('Yes, they ARE, Laya'), if you could eat paper ('Yes, you CAN, Lexi'), etc. But sometimes the girls sounded a lot like Demi and me having an argument.

When Lexi screamed, 'SHUT UP, THAT'S STUPID!' for example.

Or when Laya said, 'Bloody hell, Lexi. Ups sake, Lexi.' (Translation: 'For fuck's sake, Lexi.')

At first, I wondered where they'd got these horrible words. What an awful, disrespectful way to talk.

Probably they'd picked up things at nursery. Or from Grandad.

'Face it,' said Demi. 'They've learned those words from us.'

'Oh, that's just STUPID,' I replied.

Uh-oh.

It was true.

The kids were parroting our arguments. Mimicking our conflict. Speaking to each other with no respect.

This was all Demi's fault. He was the one who swore.

(Demi: 'You swear ALL the time!')

I informed Demi that he must not talk to me in a disrespectful manner or use swear words. With immediate effect.

He informed me that I must stop giving his things away to charity without asking, putting things in the laundry basket that were actually quite clean because I couldn't be bothered to hang them up, drink glasses of water he'd poured for himself, delete unwatched episodes of *Match of the Day*, buy new furniture when there was nothing wrong with the old stuff . . . and a bunch of other petty nonsense that I simply ignored.

We did try for a while to talk in a constructive, respectful way. But honestly – it took so much time. Far easier to just shout, 'Demi, WHY have you put all these charging leads in the drawer that is CLEARLY a tools drawer? AND THIS CHARGER IS NOW OBSOLETE ANYWAY. IT IS A STUPID PLACE TO PUT IT.'

And quicker for Demi to grumble, 'For fuck's sake.'

The girls smiling after winning a cookie competition Nana had entered them in. (Note the Laya-inflicted wound on Lexi's nose.) Shortly after this, they attacked each other.

#31 LIE – CAMPING IS A LOW-COST FAMILY HOLIDAY

As the summer sun shone brighter, reality hit me: this would be our last summer with Lexi before she started school.

We needed to make this the best summer ever. A super-duper, outdoor spectacular.

Before I had kids, I wasn't keen on the outdoors. At least, not without some sort of alcoholic drink to warm the cockles.

As a child, my sister and I were often thrown into the wild British countryside on family camping trips.

We hated these joyless 'holidays', which began with a six-hour drive up north to some freezing-cold campsite in the Pennines.

My parents would ooh and aah at the beautiful mountains and fresh-water streams, but Cath and I didn't care. We were tasteless eighties kids and wanted arcade games, mini discos and roller-skating rinks.

'The water here is so fresh!' my parents would enthuse as they encouraged us to paddle in the campsite's sub-zero stream. They would leave us to get blue feet while setting up the family tent – a 1970s beast of a thing weighing 40kg, with fifty steel poles and yards of heavy orange tarpaulin.

The tent was a real feat of structural engineering and took two hours to put up *every* time, accompanied by angry shouting about which pole went where, and then the inevitable panic that a crucial part was missing.

To our disappointment, my parents would always find that missing pole and we wouldn't get to go home.

When the tent was finally set up, with its jaunty paisley curtains and orange walls, it took a further hour to construct the rickety camping equipment – canvas camp beds, screw-together chairs, folding picnic tables (all orange, of course – everything was in those days).

The camping beds in particular required great physical strength to get the legs in place. It wasn't possible to set up them up without making Tom Jones 'HUH!' noises and going bright red in the face.

Because the huge frame tent took up most of the car, bedding was a low priority. Our parents bought themselves quite a nice, downy double sleeping bag, but my sis and I had nylon sleeping bags (also orange) that were thin enough to make shadow puppets through.

There were highlights. The melted Blue Riband bar with a cup of tea from a plastic flask, served on the hard shoulder during the long drive up north. The cinema trips during torrential rain downpours. The time we came home several days early because Dad woke up with frost in his hair and said it was 'just too bloody cold'.

Britain *is* so cold – especially for skinny fussy-eater kids like my sister and me. Maybe we should have had better outdoor gear, but outdoor gear didn't really exist in the 1980s. (Or if it did, my parents certainly weren't shelling out for it. My dad had a freezing childhood *up north* with nothing more than a duffel coat and a clip around the ear to keep him warm. Spend money on thermals! You need to toughen up, you great jessies!)

By the time Laya was two and Lexi was about to start school, I tolerated the outdoors somewhat. But let's not go crazy. I wouldn't, for example, do anything silly like go camping.

Then Lexi's nursery friends invited us to go camping.

Shit.

I hated camping. Right?

Mentally, I made my usual protestations, which were largely: 'I hate fucking camping. It's always so cold and uncomfortable.'

But the kids were really excited. Even little Laya, who could only just form whole sentences.

'Tent! Tent! Whoosh!'

'Please can we go, Mummy?' Lexi begged. 'All my friends will be there. It'll be like a giant sleepover. With marshmallows.'

I told Lexi piously that when we were kids, we *never* had marshmallows on camping trips. Just thin orange sleeping bags and burnt sausages. *If we were lucky.*

Anyway.

I considered the camping trip. Just considered, you understand. We had kids. Camping was a thing people did with kids. Oh, why not? Let's just try it out. When the kids realise how cold and uncomfortable it is, they'll never want to go again – marshmallows or otherwise.

I thanked our lovely new friends for inviting us and told them we'd be delighted to come, while privately dreading it.

Since we didn't have a stick of camping equipment, I took Lexi and Laya to the big Go Outdoors store to browse tents and so forth.

My, camping equipment was *expensive* these days. Did we really need a tent that size? It was only one weekend. Surely such a short trip didn't necessitate hundreds of pounds on camping gear? No wonder my parents bought us those thin sleeping bags – the downy ones cost a fortune.

However, I did splash out on outdoor clothes for the kids, based on my mother's advice: 'There's no wrong weather, only wrong clothes.'

Nice warm fleeces and waterproof/windproof coats were lavished on the children and I made absolutely sure they were appreciated.

'When I was a child, coats were *thin*,' I informed the kids. 'This waterproof, Gore-Tex technology didn't exist in those days. If it was windy, you got cold. If it rained, you got wet.'

'We need beds too, Mummy,' Lexi instructed. 'And a cooker. And sleeping bags. And chairs.'

'We do not *need* chairs,' I insisted. 'We'll have to load them and unload them and it's only one weekend. We can just sit on the floor.'

'Grass, Mummy,' Lexi corrected. 'We'll be sitting on grass. A floor is *inside*.'

Little smart-arse.

After mentally totting up the cost of a very basic set-up, I worked out it was the same as staying in a really nice hotel for two nights. And we were only talking about a basic camping set-up – anything luxurious like an electric cool box or comfortable beds and cooking equipment would be a waste of money for one weekend.

'We're going home, kids,' I announced. 'There's no point buying and storing all this stuff for one trip. You might not even like camping. We'll just borrow Nana and Grandad's 1970s camping gear.'

Lexi's fingers lingered over a shiny new pink-dinosaur sleeping bag.

'Can't we at least get new bedding?'

'It'll just take up space in the loft,' I insisted. 'We'll probably never go camping again when you realise how horrendous it is.'

We drove to my parents' house, where I borrowed some 1970s camp beds and dusted off the old orange sleeping bags my sister and I had used as kids. Unfortunately, the old frame tent had rotted to death some years previously.

Reluctantly, we bought a new family tent. I was certain we'd have to get rid of it when the kids realised being outdoors all day and night is cold and miserable.

I tried to get our garden chairs in the back of the car but they wouldn't fit.

Never mind. As I'd told Lexi, we didn't need chairs. We'd just sit on the floor (*grass*).

After a stressful pack-up with lots of shouting about what was and wasn't important ('we NEED THREE crates of beer, kids. Your books will have to stay at home. And no, we don't have a cooker, I've just packed sandwiches and breakfast cereal'), we headed into the Norfolk countryside.

'We'll arrive at gone 6 p.m.,' I said as we chugged through country lanes, the bedding obscuring the back window. 'Better crack on with all the setting-up. Otherwise we won't be finished before dark.'

'It gets dark at 9 p.m.,' said Demi. 'It's not going to take three hours to set up.'

'It might take longer than three hours!' I said, my hands gripping the steering wheel. 'My parents took all day once and still didn't get the inner tent set up before bedtime. My sister and I had to sleep on bare grass next to the big blue gas bottles.'

'Half an hour, maximum,' said Demi. 'Tents have fibreglass poles these days. It's easy.'

I didn't say anything, but quietly I believed him to be a fool.

When we arrived at the campsite, our friends had already unpacked and set up. There was a mountain of beer crates near the unlit campfire – I'm talking maybe ten cases. It was heartening to know that everyone else was just as worried about running out of beer as we were.

'Would you like a beer?' someone offered. 'We've got ten crates between us. Better not risk running out! Ha ha ha!'

Ha ha, indeed.

The kids piled out of the car and started running around with their friends while Demi and I unpacked and argued.

Demi and I both feel ourselves to be leaders, but Demi is wrong – I'm the *real* leader, despite all his army experience.

It took about half an hour to get everything out of the car.

Now on to the serious business of setting up the family tent. I pictured Demi and me still hammering in pegs as the sun disappeared behind the horizon. However, Demi was right again – the tent took all of ten minutes to set up.

While we were pitching the tent, the kids whined, 'We're so cold, Mummy. It's *really* windy.'

It was true – the wind was picking up and ominous clouds gathered.

'Zip up your Gore-Tex and count yourself lucky,' I snapped. 'We only had thin duffel coats in our day.'

With the tent set up, Demi and I sat around the campfire with the other parents. A light rain started, but nothing to complain about – not when you're under an event shelter with a beer in one hand and a sausage in the other.

The kids complained though. We're getting *soaked* (they weren't). It's *freezing* (it wasn't).

I now understood the necessity for marshmallows on camping trips. You throw them at the children whenever they moan.

As the evening wore on and we fired up the late-night barbecue, I realised something profound. We were having a nice time. It was great being outdoors. And a campfire with marshmallows and sausages . . .

Another beer? Sure! How many are left now, ninety-five?

The kids were complaining a lot, of course. As the sun set, it did get quite chilly. The kids were also moaning about sitting on the damp grass while everyone else lorded it above us in their fancy camping chairs.

Come on, kids – toughen up. This is good fun! We'll bring chairs next time.

Did I say next time?

Yes, I think I did.

On the face of it, camping means paying quite a bit of money to live like a homeless person. But actually, it was a great excuse for getting together with a load of other adults and drinking beer around a camp-fire. My, it was fun.

Stop complaining, Lexi and Laya. Kids *love* being outdoors.

When we got home, I went right out and bought a load of good camping equipment – thermal sleeping bags, one of those self-inflating mattresses, *really* fancy chairs, wine-glass holders that stake into the ground, camping wine glasses – the whole lot.

It cost quite a bit. More than a few nights in a fancy hotel. But we couldn't stay in fancy hotels any more anyway, so what the hey.

Fun camping trip with Lexi and other beautiful children. Note the giant marshmallow. Just excessive.

#32 LIE – WHEN THEY START SCHOOL, YOU'LL GET YOUR LIFE BACK

All of a sudden, it was time for Lexi to start school.

We couldn't quite believe this was happening.

Parents of older kids always say, 'Oh, you'll blink and she'll be at school. You just wait, it goes so quickly.'

I ignored them, stuck in my own seemingly unending newborn hell. This baby stage will never end! NEVER. It is one long sleepless-night misery and doesn't go quickly.

Yet suddenly, Lexi was no longer my little baby or even my little toddler. She was a big, long thing with her own tastes (garlic is disgusting) and opinions (you know, actually, I'm not keen on yellow). And it was time for her to start school.

This felt quite unbelievable.

Demi had already bought Lexi school shoes from H&M, but I informed him these were unsuitable.

'Lexi needs *width-fitting* school shoes,' I told Demi. 'It's vital for her foot development. She'll be wearing these shoes every day.'

'Width fitting?' Demi queried. 'What's that?'

'Where they measure the length *and* width of your foot,' I said. 'For a really good fit.'

'We never had anything like that growing up,' said Demi. 'In fact, I never had new shoes. I had hand-me-downs from my sister. It made me tough, wearing pixie boots with hearts stamped all over them. And my feet are fine. Perfectly fine.'

'You have flat feet,' I pointed out. 'Fallen arches.'

'Yes, but I was born with those.'

'We have to get width-fitting school shoes,' I insisted. 'My mum ONLY EVER bought us width-fitting shoes. They're important for healthy bone development.'

I further explained that Mum believed our feet would turn into hideous, gnarled, old-hag claws if we didn't wear width-fitting shoes.

'That sounds like bollocks,' said Demi. 'A few extra millimetres? I've never met an adult with foot problems caused by childhood footwear. And what about if you have narrow feet – is it important that your shoes fit snugly at the sides? I mean, really?'

I ignored this cynicism. When it came to Lexi's first pair of school shoes, I would follow my mother's fine example.

One Saturday, Lexi and I took our first trip to Clarks shoe shop. I sold this to Lexi as a real event. A momentous life occasion, similar to buying a wedding dress. Her first pair of school shoes. And yes, Lexi, you can choose any pair of shoes you like.

I never should have said that before checking the prices.

God damn you, Lelli Kelly.

HOW much for one pair of shoes? But they're TINY. They cost more than MY shoes!

Anyway.

Once we'd purchased Lexi's extortionate shoes and had them elaborately boxed and wrapped in tissue paper, I asked the question I should have asked in the first place: 'What is a standard child's shoe width sold by, say, H&M or Primark?'

The Clarks assistant told me the 'average' shoe width was an F fitting.

'So all shoes in other shops come in F fittings?' I said.

'Yes,' said the assistant. 'That would be the standard.'

'And what width is Lexi?' I asked.

'An F,' she replied.

'So Lexi matches the width sold in every other shoe shop in the country?' I confirmed. 'Including the cheaper and cooler H&M?'

'Yes,' said the assistant. 'Although we do have a sale on. Those bright-green £50 shoes are £45 now.'

'Schools don't let kids wear green shoes.'

Still, at least we had everything we needed for Lexi's first day at school. And before we knew it, that great day was upon us – our little bird flying the nest.

The wave of emotions hit before we left the house.

'Look,' Lexi smiled, marching up and down in her new grey pinafore and red cardigan. 'I'm a grown-up schoolgirl. You be teacher. Tell me to read this book. Then shout at me for not reading right.'

Laya looked on admiringly, pulling at Lexi's red cardigan with her cuddly hands and saying, 'Pisscess' (princess).

'Not princess, Laya,' Lexi corrected, in her patient-big-sister voice. 'Schoolgirl. Big schoolgirl.'

I burst into tears.

'What's wrong, Mummy?' Lexi asked, adding a 'tra la laaa!' for good measure.

'You're leaving me,' I gulped.

'But you said you'd be happy when I started school,' said Lexi. 'You told those other mummies you couldn't wait. That you'd have lots more time. That you'd get your old life back.'

Yes, I did say that.

I'd joked about what a relief school would be. So did every other working mother I knew. 'Five days' free childcare, ho ho ho! I can't wait! Miss her? Ah, ha ha ha! I don't think so – I have far too much catching-up to do.'

It turns out this was all bravado.

As we walked up the country path, I realised that one day Lexi would leave me. Not today, but one day. She wouldn't need me any more. And I felt so sad about it, and so desperately grateful that she was in my life.

Whoa. What was happening?

I clung to Lexi at the school gates. I tried not to cry because, you know, it upsets the kids. I shared misty-eyed sad looks with other mothers, all of us experiencing our own little soap-opera moment.

Lexi's first day at school. She is delighted. I am making a big silly fuss. And she didn't even wear those expensive school shoes – she wanted wellies.

What was going on?

For someone who'd been desperate *not* to be needed every waking second, it was the most ridiculous turnaround. Wasn't I always bleating on about independence? Telling Lexi how great it was to do things for herself and not bother poor, tired Mummy who had just sat down with a cup of tea (and a bag of M&Ms secretly stashed under the cushion).

Independence is not neglect! Wasn't that one of my catchphrases?

When Lexi was born, I longed for a break. Just one teeny-tiny day off. It was all so relentless – every hour of every day with a dependant. Yes, yes, she was lovely. With her lovely little head! Aww . . .

But there is no sidestepping or skiving when you have a baby. No computer program to do all the hard work for you. No sick days. No bank holidays. All day, every day, and nights too. Breastfeeding boobs don't have days off.

I longed for the days when the kids would be old enough to take care of themselves.

But I didn't long for those days right now.

It had finally hit me.

I was happy having the kids around. Really, really happy. It had just taken me five years to realise it.

Yes, I was tired sometimes. Yes, I got bored pretending all those pages of scribbles were works of genius. No, I didn't want to load the dishwasher again. But I loved having a family, I really did. The kids were part of me and I was part of them.

Now my firstborn was being ripped away from me into the cold, hard clutches of school . . .

I decided right there and then to embrace the moment and every moment from now on in. To truly live my life, not wish for another one. And with that decision (a decision I should have made a long time ago) came more freedom and joy than I'd ever known.

When I chose to appreciate what I had, I realised I was in love every day and my heart was full to bursting point.

I only needed the kids, Demi, our friends and a few family-friendly activities to overflow with happiness.

I hadn't meant to. I hadn't wanted to. I hadn't realised it would happen. But through a process of pain and the crushing to death of my old self, I'd finally entered the next stage of life and become happy.

We were on the family roller coaster, and for once I actually didn't want to get off.

It was time to stop complaining and start enjoying the ride.

#33 LIE – KIDS ARE PORTABLE, YOU CAN TAKE THEM ANYWHERE

With Lexi settled into school and Christmas on its way, we planned a city trip to catch up with old friends.

When we left Brighton, we assumed we'd come back often. In fact, I'd been certain we'd move back there within a few years. After all, we loved the city, right? All the fun, creative stuff and good food? But somehow, with the chaos of the move, the new baby, the house renovations, Lexi starting school . . . well, we'd never made it back.

The kids would love it, we decided. They'd slot right into the big city. Kids are portable, right? And it was *Christmas* time. Magico! Kids enjoy everything at this time of year, right?

We strapped the kids into the sensible family car, packed a jolly picnic in our sensible cool bag (those roadside places cost a fortune) and set off to the very unsensible bright Christmas lights of Brighton.

It would be exciting, wouldn't it?

I asked Lexi if she remembered our old home in Brighton.

She tried for, 'The carpet was orange?'

It wasn't.

'Do you remember your Italian childminder, Mama Marzia?' I prompted. 'She used to say *ciao, bella.*'

Lexi couldn't remember, and further disappointed us with her poor Italian pronunciation.

'Not *chew berry*, Lexi. *Ciao, bella.*'

As we drove on, we reminisced about our life in Brighton. We talked about all the pubs we used to go to, the clubs on the beach and that late-night hidden cocktail lounge above the Theatre Royal – the one with the speakeasy feel that would only let you in if you had friends in the theatre.

We obviously couldn't do a pub crawl with the kids in tow (Or could we? No, best not), but we were excited about the sushi restaurants, cupcake bakeries and cool vintage-clothes shopping. Maybe we could fit in a bit of Christmas shopping. Buy some quirky homewares.

As we drove into Brighton, our hearts lifted at all the colourful, creative sights.

How we'd missed those fresh croissants and multi-coloured meringues!

There were bright neon Christmas lights everywhere and artistic festive displays.

'So, who have we arranged to meet up with?' I asked Demi.

'No one exactly,' said Demi. 'Panda and Jim are the only people who live in the city centre now, and they're visiting family for Christmas.'

'What about Roxy and Dave and their partners? They still live in the suburbs, don't they?'

'Yes, but there's a chickenpox thing going around,' said Demi. 'It's not a good weekend.'

It never is when you have kids.

We drove right into Brighton and headed for one of the city-centre car parks. Goodness me, driving is convenient, I thought. I'm so glad we bought this car. We really did need a family vehicle.

Then I saw the city parking fees.

£30 for the day!

No wonder we never had a car when we lived here.

Sure, I wasn't so worried about money these days. But there was no point *throwing* it away.

An outraged drive around the city centre followed, narrated by me channelling my mother: 'We're not paying that much for parking! It's outrageous! We could all go to the cinema for the same price!'

Finally, I discovered what looked to be a parking spot somewhat out of the city centre.

'Come on, kids,' I announced. 'It's just a short walk from here. Your dad and I used to live around the corner.'

Of course, with kids, nothing is a short walk. Especially when it's actually quite a long walk.

'The city is so crowded,' I said as we were bumped and jostled by Christmas shoppers. 'Hey. HEY! Watch where you're going, you in the Santa suit – you just shoved my small child out of the way, you twat! Lexi, WATCH THAT CAR!'

Everyone was young, cool, fashionable and child-free. Some of the girls (and boys) wore perfectly applied, retro-red lipstick *in the middle of the day*. The middle of the day!

Who had the time for that sort of effort?

In contrast, I wore peddle-pusher jeans, white plimsolls and a striped T-shirt. My hair wasn't long any more, just tidy in layers. There were no peacock-like red or blonde streaks. And I was just, well, older.

Demi looked like a normal (very cool) dad.

(Demi: 'I wore the same clothes I'd worn before we had Lexi. How can you improve on perfection?')

Everyone on the streets of Brighton looked great. But spending time and money on your appearance is a young man's game. The sort of thing you do when you have free time and money. And, to be honest, it all seemed a world away from our love-filled life with kids.

Twenty-somethings fell out of pubs, clasping festive cocktail glasses and wearing ironic Christmas jumpers. Some drank cups of mulled wine mid-morning. Had we ever done such a thing? It was so irresponsible!

'Are you sure children are allowed here, Mummy?' Lexi asked in that hushed whisper she reserved for my more mega parental failings. 'There are no other children. Have you got it wrong again? Like when you tried to take me around that whiskey museum and they said I had to be over eighteen and you shouted?'

'Of course children are allowed,' I insisted. 'There must be some other children here. Ah. There. See? That woman is carrying a child in a sling.'

'That's a baby,' said Lexi. 'What about *kids*?'

We kept looking, but saw only harassed-looking new parents with very young babies strapped to their bodies.

'I suppose the city isn't really for kids,' I said. 'Even at Christmas. It *is* quite crowded.'

'Then why are we here?'

'It'll be fun! Did I tell you about the amazing curry restaurant?'

'Restaurants aren't for kids, Mummy. We need a park.'

'There isn't one nearby. Not in the middle of the city. How about the library? You like a library.'

We continued our difficult walk towards Brighton library, passing colourful ice-cream parlours, cupcake 'factories' and brightly coloured, extortionately priced toy shops.

'Mu-um . . . can we have—?'

'No!'

When we reached the library, it was closed.

'It's 10 a.m. on a Saturday,' I raged. 'Why on earth isn't it open?'

'Everyone's probably still in bed,' said Demi. 'Sleeping off their hangovers.'

Unperturbed, we headed to a trendy coffee shop and perched the kids on dangerous bar stools while Demi and I joined the huge queue.

'You can't have your buggy in here,' the coffee-shop girl shouted across the tastefully beaten-up wood counter.

'Oh. Sorry. Where should we put it then?'

'In a different coffee shop. This one isn't for kids.'

Right.

Point taken.

We dragged the kids around for a few more hours, fielding requests for ice cream and expensive Hello Kitty items, and finally it was near enough 12 p.m. to justify having lunch.

We headed for a fun sushi-train restaurant and watched our kids knock sushi plates off the conveyor belt while we apologised over and over again. And shouted at the kids, 'BE MORE CAREFUL. EACH TINY PLATE COSTS £3 OR MORE!'

Waitresses and customers glared at us.

No one smiled at the kids or brought them crayons.

We spent the rest of the afternoon wandering around, wondering what on earth there was to do.

The kids weren't interested in buying artistic Christmas decorations, and that colourful sex shop was obviously right out. Save for a two-minute mince-pie fix here and there, what was there for a family in the city?

We decided to check out our hotel a bit early. It was a boutique, modern place boasting cool pod-like bedrooms and coloured Perspex everywhere (and a special deal that weekend – hence the choice).

The reception staff were not pleased to see us.

'You have children,' said the French-accented reception man. 'That will be difficult.'

'Why?' I asked.

'We have live bands playing this evening. Until one a.m.'

The mystery of the 'special deal' hotel room was solved.

'I did write on the reservation that we had two kids with us,' I said. 'And we booked a three-bed room with a cot.'

'A cot?' The man looked bewildered.

'Yes,' I said. 'A travel cot. You do have a travel cot, don't you?'

'I'll see what we can find.'

An hour later, following a hysterical meltdown by the reception man ('I do not know this thing! We do not have it!'), we finally agreed just to use a folded-over duvet on the floor as a kiddie bed. This meant watching Laya vigilantly until she fell asleep – and praying she wouldn't fiddle with the radiators in her sleep.

Finally, over the *thump-thump-thump* of a live band playing 'Fairy Tale in New York', the kids drifted off.

'We should have a drink,' said Demi. 'Live it up a bit.'

'There's a minibar,' I said, trying to muster some excitement. 'We can drink mini spirit bottles in a dark hotel room, trying not to talk too loudly.'

Demi dutifully checked out the minibar.

'There are miniature whiskeys,' he announced. 'And miniature gin.'

'How much are they?' I asked.

'£7 each.'

'You could buy a whole bottle of gin for the same price as two miniatures. There's a supermarket over the road.'

'Fine.' Demi gave a long-suffering sigh. 'So you want me to go to the supermarket?'

'Yes, please.'

Demi brought back a full-sized bottle of chilled white wine, and I commented on the pleasing high standard of alcohol refrigeration in the big city.

We slugged wine from the bottle because we weren't sure if we were allowed to use the minibar glassware. There was no room in the minibar fridge for a full-sized bottle either, so the wine was soon room temperature in our hot hands.

As we were drinking warm wine from the bottle, my mum called.

The children stirred, and I felt irritated. Didn't Mum know we were in a dark room with sleeping children? Why wasn't she telepathic?

'Surprise!' said Mum. 'We're in Brighton.'

'*Mum*,' I hissed. 'We're in a dark room with sleeping children and – hang on a minute. You're where?'

'Brighton! Your dad and I were visiting friends in Lewes today, so we thought – we're so nearby, let's surprise you in Brighton and offer some babysitting.'

I felt very bad about being irritated.

'Thanks so much, Mum,' I said. 'That's really thoughtful and nice.'

They're like that, my parents. Very thoughtful and nice. Except when they're not looking after my kids *exactly* as I tell them to. Then we have arguments.

'Demi,' I whispered. 'My parents are in Brighton. They're offering to babysit.'

'They're wonderful,' he said.

'Yes, they are.'

'So we can go out then?'

'Yes. If you want to. Do you want to?'

We thought about it. Did we want to go out into the busy, noisy city? Not really. But every parent knows it's silly to turn down free babysitting.

'Thanks, Mum,' I said. 'We'd love to go out for a bit. We're sitting in a dark hotel room right now.'

'Oh, I remember those days,' said Mum. 'Trying to keep quiet. Praying the phone doesn't ring. What time do you want us there?'

Half an hour later, my parents arrived and were welcomed to our hotel room with hugs and thanks.

We handed my parents a warm, half-drunk bottle of wine and told them to help themselves to the minibar – but not to go too mad, since spirits cost £7.

Then we headed down to the fizzy, exciting streets of Brighton as two child-free people, able to see and do whatever we liked.

There was so much visual stimulation – brightly designed shop fronts, so many people in ironic Christmas jumpers, bars spilling out on to the pavement and input, input, input.

It was a lot for our tired brains to cope with.

And it felt weird without the kids. Like a limb was missing.

'Shall we just have one drink in a nice, quiet pub?' I said. 'Then get back to the children?'

'Good idea,' said Demi. 'Which pub?'

The thing with frenetic, creative big cities is that night spots are always changing hands. Nothing stays the same for long, and those places you used to know soon transform into something else.

And truth be told, there isn't really such a thing as a quiet pub in a city on a Saturday night. Just a slightly less noisy pub.

We opted for the Basket Makers, which is a traditional sort of place with cigarette tins nailed to the walls. It was rammed, with a three-person-deep queue for the bar.

'Was it always this busy?' I asked Demi.

'Probably,' he said. 'But we were too young and drunk to care.'

I kept waiting to bump into someone we knew, but there was no one.

'I hope the kids are OK,' I said. 'It'll be weird if they wake up, seeing my parents there. They won't know what's going on.'

'I miss the kids too,' said Demi. 'Let's go back and watch them sleeping.'

At 9.30 p.m. we decided to call it a night.

'You're back soon,' Mum said when we returned to the hotel. 'Didn't you have a good time?'

'Not really,' I said. 'It was all a bit frantic. We'd rather go out to a nice quiet pub back home. Or a friend's house.'

When my parents left, Demi and I toyed with raiding the minibar and making some sort of cocktail invention. After all, we'd saved quite a bit on our 'half a night out'. But truthfully, all we really wanted to do was go to sleep, wake up early with the kids, and head home.

Yes, home. Our real home. This place wasn't our home any more.

As loud music thumped through the hotel floor, I realised where we are is so much better for families. People smile in the street and say hello. Our neighbours bring us plant seeds and fruit cake. We can leave the front door unlocked and the buggy in the garden and not worry about it. No one rushes around or throws up on the pavement. The post office has no queue.

In the city, we'd been 'Pretty Womaned' every time we brought the kids into a cafe.

'No, sorry – we don't have highchairs. Fuck off with your baby.'

Brighton definitely wasn't home any more. I didn't feel connected to the city at all. This was the life we used to have. But we were different now.

'We don't fit here,' I told Demi.

'No,' said Demi. 'But that's OK, isn't it?'

'Better than OK. It's great.'

The next day, we packed up and drove home.

Life had changed. Forever.

It wasn't a question of waiting until the kids were a bit older then slotting back into our big-city, party lifestyle.

We were different. Life was different. There was no going back.

'Did you like our little city break?' I asked Lexi.

'It was OK,' said Lexi.

'Which bit did you like the best?' I asked.

'Nana giving us chocolate.'

'What?' I blinked rapidly. '*What?* When did Nana give you chocolate? You didn't see Nana – surely? You were sleeping.'

'She woke us up,' said Lexi. 'And said we could have a midnight feast from the minibar.'

'Midnight feast!' Laya concurred.

'What sort of chocolate?' I asked, trying to remember the minibar prices. 'Was it triangle-shaped (£5 Toblerone) or round (£10 Ferrero Rocher)?'

'Round.'

I quelled my outrage at Mum giving out chocolate at bedtime and patted Lexi's soft little hand.

'Well, we can have chocolate at home now.'

'Will we move back to Brighton one day?' Lexi asked as we pulled into our driveway. 'Like you said?'

'When did I say that?' I asked.

'You said when your books did well, we'd move back to Brighton.'

'I did used to say that,' I remembered as we headed into our house. 'But I was wrong. The city isn't the life for us any more. This is where we belong.'

The kids went out and played in the garden.

Demi and I planned a roast dinner. We picked fresh blackberries to make a crumble.

Everything felt peaceful and quiet and easy.

Life . . . It *felt* great. More than great.

It felt happily ever after.

TRUTH – WE WOULDN'T CHANGE IT FOR THE WORLD

Christmas was on its way, and I decided to clear out the last vestiges of our former life. All that novelty, studenty party crap I hadn't had the courage to chuck out before. The stuff I thought we just might use again.

I gave the kids and Demi huge bin bags, and we went around the house bagging up anything that hadn't been used, hung or unboxed since we moved.

We threw out the branded Jack Daniels shot glasses, the pineapple sunglasses and the giant plushy St Patrick's Day hat. We threw out old CDs and mix tapes, music magazines and novelty inflatable chairs. My beaten-up old backpack. Anything that didn't fit our life right now, out it went.

No longer did we straddle the great divide between youth and parenthood. We knew exactly who we were and who we wanted to be.

We drove to the tip in our big family car, and the kids had fun chucking novelty party goods in the big metal containers.

I watched the final remnants of our pre-child life join the big piles of rubbish. It was a relief now, letting that stuff go. Clubbing until the sun came out. Child-free brunches at 11 a.m. Interrailing holidays and backpacking around Asia. It was great at the time, but it wasn't who we were any more.

We didn't miss it.

We were far too happy.

'Mummy,' Lexi asked as we looked into the cavernous metal skip, 'are all these things dead now?'

'They were already dead,' I told her. 'They've been dead for a long time.'

Parenthood comes with suffering.

First there is letting go of what is. The ripping-apart of the old life, never to be sewn back together.

I will never again spend a day happily getting drunk in a field, with no responsibilities or cares of what will happen tomorrow. I will never again wear anything tight around the stomach. I will never trek across Thailand with only a backpack, wearing teeny-tiny shorts and covered in neon full-moon-party paint.

Then there is the hard work. Waking up at the crack of dawn every day, seven days a week. Cooking three meals a day for little people. Washing aforementioned little people and cutting all those fingernails and toenails.

Finally, there is the acceptance of what *is*: love, service, happiness, community, friends and contentment.

We can't stay young forever. Kids mean growing up and, as painful as that can be, it's good for us.

Demi and I had suffered. We'd been forced into a life that felt terrifying, exhausting and relentless. But we had grown.

Life, which had once been solely about us, now revolved around kids, a house and family. And do you know what? Once we stopped fighting it, we found more happiness than we'd ever known.

As Christmas approached, Demi and I reminisced about our parenting journey.

We were so far removed from those youthful, child-free people who'd lived in Brighton and played the Dolphin Derby on the pier every weekend (probably while holding a pint of cider). We didn't look the same, do the same things, or feel or think the same way.

Now we lived in a family home in the countryside and spent time walking slowly while answering the many necessary questions of small children.

'Why is that tree there? Why do I have to hurry up? Why can't I run out in front of that fast-moving removal truck? Muuuuum. Mummmm. Answer me! It IS a sensible question, Mummy!'

You know the sort of thing.

Of course, things weren't perfect. Not by a long chalk. Laya had diarrhoea at the school Christmas fair, for example, which was bad.

If you've never been to a school Christmas fair, I have one word for you: don't.

They are chaotic, sugar-fuelled events full of screaming, overexcited kids demanding parents buy second-hand 1980s board games ('Build a Better Burger' or 'Perfection', anyone?).

Suffice it to say, it's not easy to reach a toilet when you're swimming in the choppy waters of sugar-fuelled children.

But perfect is boring. In all the chaos and (sometimes literal) crap of parenthood, we enjoyed ourselves and embraced the family-friendly festive season.

This Christmas, I was determined to do things properly.

We had emerged from house renovations and newborn chaos, toddler chaos, more newborn chaos, more toddler chaos and now finally had time and energy to DO Christmas with a capital 'D' (and O, it turns out).

We would have a high old festive time as a family and turn our home into a glittery, sparkly seasonal delight, complete with fresh holly from the local woods, handmade paper chains and cookies hung on the Christmas tree.

The kids would love it. So would we.

◆ ◆ ◆

On Christmas Eve, Demi and I woke to the screams and hoots of two small children, leaping around the place.

'It's Christmas Eve, Laya!'

'Christmas Eve, Lexi.'

'Magico!'

'Magico!'

'What are we doing today, Mummy?' Lexi asked. 'It's Christmas Eve. Magico!'

It was indeed magico.

Demi and I both had the day off. A day of family fun awaited us – and, better still, we were really looking forward to it.

Lexi and Laya's eyes were full of wonder when we told them about the big fat man who would magically squeeze himself down the chimney that evening.

Lexi helpfully explained away all the Santa plot holes for her little sister.

'Well, he *can visit* the children without chimneys, Laya, because he has a magic key to all the houses.'

As a family, we decided to do the following:

- Collect fresh holly from the woods to decorate the house
- Make Christmas cookies
- Watch *Home Alone* and pop popcorn

The kids were sooo excited. Demi and I were sooo happy and thankful for our life.

We were right smug bastards.

OK, so it would be nice if the kids woke up a bit later, had eaten the healthy breakfast I made, and hadn't left a trail of Disney DVDs and fancy-dress items around the house. But all in all, life was good.

I no longer looked like a dishevelled winter hobo, as I had the year Lexi was born. I'd embraced looser jeans, brightly coloured tops, Converse, wool coats, scarves and knee-high leather boots. I got rid of the home-dyed streaks in my hair and had an actual adult hairstyle. My skin was a lot better, since we now got an organic vegetable bag and cooked our own meals. And of course, I was smiling a lot. That's always a good look.

Better still, we no longer lived in an orange-and-brown one-bedroom old-lady flat, piled high with baby detritus and second-hand (or stolen) furniture. We had a proper family home with beautiful modern furniture we'd actually paid for, including a huge dining table and an American-style fridge with kids' pictures all over it. The downstairs was big and open-plan with plenty of room for a massive Christmas tree and presents. We had a fireplace to hang the stockings, and front and back gardens strung with Christmas lights.

In short, our life sparkled with Christmas magic.

The kids enjoying our house at Christmas time. Look – no orange wallpaper!

If you'd shoved us into this life five years ago, we would have found it horrendous.

'What's that? I can't even leave the *house* when I want? But what if we run out of milk? I have to take these kids with me *everywhere*? But that will take ages . . . and you're saying I have to do this every single day?'

We may have decided not to bother with kids at all.

But we would have been wrong.

Totally wrong.

So we headed into the woods, laughing and joking and pretending to be dragons and chasing the kids.

We cut holly for the mantelpiece, stopped Laya attacking people with the giant shears, then finally wrestled her to the ground and took them from her.

Back home, we cut and tied the holly into bunches for our mantelpiece and roasted some chestnuts.

We made Christmas bird cakes for the robins hopping around our garden, and hung an elaborate, messy wreath on our front door. We baked Christmas cookies (from a packet, admittedly). The cookies were a bit misshapen and the wreath full of spider webs, but it was fine – the kids had fun.

We were like a John Lewis advert, except our clothes probably needed more ironing.

That afternoon, we sat with the kids, eating misshapen Christmas cookies then had a Christmas-inspired turkey and cranberry-sauce pizza for tea (mistake) and mince-pie ice cream (actually quite nice). Then we lit the wood-burning stove, sat on the big sofa (big enough for four people now) under our big, leopard-print, snuggly blanket and watched a family Christmas movie that Demi claimed made him feel physically sick.

Demi and I had a few glasses of sherry.

It was the perfect day, made even more perfect by the fact we had many more years with the kids to come.

Before bed, we let the kids lay out food and drink for Santa – casually steering them towards the things Demi and I wanted to eat and drink.

'I think Santa would like a nice cold glass of Prosecco this year, wouldn't he? And one of those Marks & Spencer all-butter, double-chocolate cookies for Rudolph? He'll be sick of carrots . . . no, it's fine. Reindeers can eat wheat. They don't have intolerances like your friend at school. And yes, chocolate is fine for them too. No, it won't poison Rudolph. You're thinking about dogs . . .'

We hung the oversized stockings above the fireplace, accompanied by the sort of speech my mum used to give about how Santa gives a *lot* these days – too much really – and how when we were growing up we had a *normal*-sized stocking containing one *small* present, a satsuma and a walnut.

When the kids became tired to the point of irritating, we packed them off to bed and watched *Die Hard*. Then we had a nice early night, smug in the knowledge that tomorrow morning we wouldn't be hungover like all those young child-free people.

'Do you remember our first Christmas with Lexi?' I asked Demi.

Demi nodded, his face turning white. 'Ugh. Yes. It was awful. We didn't know what we were doing, did we? And you were so anxious.'

'No, I wasn't!'

I was, but . . . you know, it's a bit like when people say bad things about your parents. I can say it, but *you* can't.

On Christmas Day, our house was warm and Christmassy and twinkling with magical lights (which might have been a fire hazard left on overnight, now I think about it . . .).

Stockings were placed at the end of the kids' beds. Santa's empty Prosecco glass sat by the wood-burning stove and Rudolph's cookie was nothing but crumbs.

Gleaming presents from 'Santa' waited for the kids under the tree: a Play-Doh Hair Salon for Laya and ill-advised roller skates for Lexi. (We tried to persuade her that roller skates are harder than they look – she fell over many times on Christmas morning.)

I woke up before the kids (5 a.m.) and made myself a nice cup of tea, enjoying our Christmassy house and the peace and quiet. I thought about that first Christmas as a new parent, when bats had beaten their wings in my chest (writers are so dramatic, aren't they?) and I'd felt so lonely and afraid.

I thought about how far we'd come and how happy we were. How having kids had been the hardest journey, but also the best decision we'd ever made.

Then the kids woke up.

Bloody hell.

Why couldn't they sleep a little bit longer? WHY? It was only 5 a.m. for goodness' sake . . .

'Mummy, Mummy, Mummy, Christmas DAAAAAAAY!'

Still, nice to see their excited little faces.

'Hey, kids!' I enthused. 'Have you seen your stockings? They're on your beds. Santa leaves them there so you STAY IN YOUR BEDROOMS and open them before you wake your dad up. He gets grumpy when he's tired. That's why Santa does stockings. To give the parents a longer rest.'

'But you're up already—'

'I'm relaxing!'

'Why do YOU need to relax. Dad does all the cooking—'

'I do plenty!'

'A cheeseboard isn't cooking.'

'YES, IT IS!'

After two minutes of stocking distraction, the kids came piling into our bedroom and jumped on our bed.

'Santa, Santa, Santa!'

Demi put on his Santa onesie and jumped up and down on the bed too.

'Santa, Santa!'

'Can everyone PLEASE KEEP STILL!' I shouted. 'I'm holding a hot cup of tea!'

At 5.05 a.m. we succumbed to the children's request to come downstairs and open their big presents.

'Isn't it funny?' Lexi laughed. 'Santa uses the same wrapping paper as we do!'

Yes. Hilarious. But don't think too much about it . . .

I attempted special eggs Benedict for breakfast, but ended up with swirls of egg white in a pan of boiling water.

Poaching an egg is impossible. Absolutely impossible.

Luckily, the kids hadn't wanted eggs Benedict anyway and happily settled for 'Christmas' Coco Pops (Coco the Monkey was holding a holly sprig on the cereal box, so you know . . . a festive breakfast).

Demi kindly stepped in and made eggs and bacon while playing reggae Christmas songs.

We had fun.

The Buddha says the path to enlightenment is paved with many little deaths.

When Lexi was born it sometimes felt like life had ended.

It was true – a life had ended.

But another was just beginning.

It had happened. After five long years of parenthood, we had finally become parents.

And we wouldn't change it for the world.

Family happiness. We have a lot of fun with these little girls. Wouldn't change 'em. Well, you can't, can you? No – that's a joke, girls. We really honestly wouldn't change you.

THANK YOU for finishing my book.

I love you ever so much.

If you have a minute, PLEASE write a review.

I read ALL my Amazon and Goodreads reviews (yes, the bad ones do make me cry) and good reviews mean EVERYTHING.

Reviews don't have to be fancy. In fact, just one word is great (as long as it isn't 'shit' . . .). And they do more good than you could ever imagine.

So GO AHEAD and review – I would LOVE to see what you have to say.

I'm a chatty sort and LOVE talking to readers. If you want to ask me any questions about the book or talk about anything at all, get in touch:

Email: suzykquinn@devoted-ebooks.com

Facebook.com/suzykquinn (You can friend-request me. I like friends.)

Twitter: @suzykquinn

Also, I got me a **website**: www.suzykquinn.com

Suzy Xxx

FREE ROMANTIC COMEDY STARTER LIBRARY

Free book download, cover reveals and launch news when you sign up for my newsletter at

WWW.SUZYKQUINN.COM/SUZYNEWS

ABOUT THE AUTHOR

Suzy K Quinn is a British fiction author, and writes in three different genres: psychological thriller, comedy and romance.

She was first published by Hachette in 2010 with her debut novel *Glass Geishas* (now *Night Girls*), then self-published a romance series, the Ivy Lessons, which became an international bestseller, selling half a million copies and becoming a #1 Kindle romance bestseller in the US and UK.

After her second daughter was born, she self-published the Bad Mother's Diary series, which also became a #1 Kindle bestseller.

Suzy K Quinn's novels have been translated into seven languages and her books have sold over three quarters of a million copies worldwide.

Suzy lives in Wivenhoe, Essex, with her husband Demi and two daughters. She would love another baby but her pelvic floor says no.

www.suzykquinn.com
www.facebook.com/suzykquinn
Twitter: @suzykquinn